# Spoked Dreams
## An Odyssey by Bicycle and Mind

Charles Riddel

**Air-Space Press**
Austin, Texas
www.air-spacepress.com

*Spoked Dreams—An Odyssey by Bicycle and Mind*

Published by Air-Space Press

First Edition/First Printing


ISBN 10:  0-9770593-0-8
ISBN 13: 978-0-9770593-0-0


All photos by the author

Illustrations by Elizabeth A. Day

Cover Design by Blake Mitchell


Air-Space Press
P.O. Box 152739
Austin, Texas 78715-2739

www.air-spacepress.com


Printed in the United States of America
at Morgan Printing in Austin, Texas

# Table of Contents

## Waypoints and High Points

1. First High Pass - 8,406 ft.
2. Capitol Reef National Park
3. Crossing Lake Powell
4. Natural Bridges National Park
5. Arches National Park
6. Canyonlands National Park
7. Chaco Canyon
8. Coal Bank Pass
9. Molas Pass
10. Red Mountain Pass
11. Dallas Divide
12. Lizard Head Pass
13. Four Corners Monument
14. Monument Valley
15. Little Colorado River
16. Sunset Crater National Monument
17. Lowell Observatory
18. Oak Creek Canyon
19. Clear Creek
20. Morman Lake
21. Humphrey's Peak
22. Grand Canyon
23. Jump to Lake Mead
24. Mountain Springs Summit
25. Salsbury Pass
26. Bad Water - Death Valley
27. Emigrant Pass
28. Wild Rose Pass
29. Walker Pass
30. Pine Mountain Summit

Bike Route

Auto shuttle

NEVADA / CALIFORNIA

UTAH / NAVADA

SIERRA NEVADA

Death Valley

**27** 190
Furnace Creek Ranch
**28**
**29**
**26**
Pahrump
**25** 160
178
Shoshone
**24**
Las Vegas
Lake Meade
**23**
93

Ridgecrest

Bodfish
**Bakersfield**
Maricopa 166
Arvin
**Santa Barbara** 33
**30**

PACIFIC OCEAN

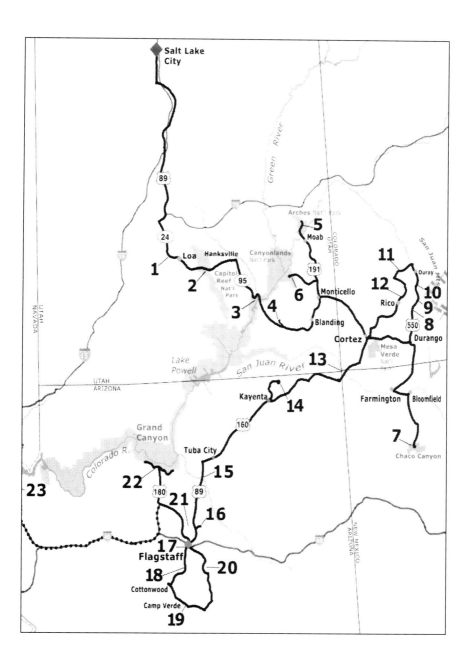

# Preface

Some things are greater than the sum of the parts. This was one of those things.

*Spoked Dreams* tells the story of a solo bicycle trip that spanned sixty-six days and included 2,509 miles of riding and over 200 miles of hiking through six southwestern states. The numbers, the route, and a list of places seen do not capture the experience of doing it. *Spoked Dreams* is not a travel guide or a "how-to" book although it contains good information for anyone contemplating an extended bicycle trip. *Spoked Dreams* is mostly about the experience of the ride, and its real story is about riding from one place in *life* to another.

The details of the experience were recorded in my journal, in the letters that I wrote, in the many photographs that I took and in memories that are, in some cases, still so vivid that I can close my eyes and be in the midst of the ride. The story is told from the perspective of that time, back in 1980, as recorded by all these things.

Before conceiving this bicycle trip, I had traveled extensively throughout the region by vehicle, hiking and camping. I questioned whether or not a bicycle trip would be worthwhile given all of my previous visits. But I learned that trimming down to a minimal load, simplifying, and crossing distances normally associated with motorized conveyance, relying upon my own power instead, dramatically changes one's perspective of both the land and life. I discovered some new places as well as some details I had previously overlooked in old places. And I discovered that disconnecting from the constant conveyor belt of the modern world opens a door to new connections that are profoundly relevant. The story is not all about what I saw, but also how I saw it.

This book celebrates what is accessible. I was not a gifted athlete, nor a serious cyclist. I used ordinary equipment and rode an ordinary bike. I ate ordinary food that I could find in little stores in the outback. I didn't spend a lot of money and the minimal training I did was sandwiched into my ordinary routine. I did not travel to an exotic land but found one not too far from home. Mostly, this trip required letting go for a while—letting go of all the excuses not to devote just a couple of months out of years to explore new limits.

Although it is a personal journal, I have attempted to make *Spoked Dreams* about things other than me, focusing on the experience of the trip and the discoveries revealed.

At the time I made this trip in 1980, I also decided to leave Austin, the city that had been my home for eight years, and to leave Texas, the state that had been my home for my entire life. I planned to test life in Santa Barbara, a city that I had never visited and had picked from a California almanac. This uprooting made my "disconnect" somewhat more absolute and probably deepened the spell of my journey. But the choice to give up the vehicle, the radio, the television, the newspaper, the watch, the calendar, the set itinerary, and the expectations of others was far more significant. In the final analysis, only one decision really mattered, the decision to ride, because the details of the ride were mostly spontaneous.

Although the rugged landscapes are essentially the same today, other things have changed since I made my meandering journey from high desert to ocean. Some of the waypoints are barely recognizable. Some of the highways have taken on a different character or their names have changed. Cell phones can now penetrate the isolation and summon friendly voices or help in emergencies. The crowds are now bigger in many places. And yes, there are even more bicyclists these days. It's harder to be physically alone, today—even though loneliness can envelop a person in the midst of a city. True then. True now. Personally verified.

I am more weathered now, tested in ways that I never anticipated or wanted. Life can be harsh. But something from my long, lonesome bicycle ride remains with me today—lessons about pedaling, about recognizing hidden mysteries, and about the value of simple things that are truly amazing when fully considered. The indelible afterglow of the journey occasionally saves me—much as the ride did then.

# 1. The Call

I was awake that summer.

The ceiling vanished. I saw cobalt skies and tangerine sunsets. The floor turned to rutted sandstone. The walls were layered with a succession of plateaus.

I rode the bike path around Town Lake in ten-mile segments. In thought, I laid them end to end—connected them into sixty-mile vaults across painted deserts.

I taught calculus by day. I stared at the walls by night. Wide-eyed and restless, I parted the curtains to reveal the only distance not caged by the city, the moon hanging from a featureless sky. Moonlight swept my room, brushed the large topographic map of Canyonlands above my bed, and illuminated the faint sadness that paced around within me. I circled, locked up and peering through the bars of my routine, tiptoeing along imaginary treks on dotted-line trails that switched back across the contour lines inked upon the map.

It wasn't an inspiration. It was a realization, a yearning.

"It's out there. . ."

It wasn't a decision. It was a necessity.

"It's out there—somewhere. . ."

The call whispered from the gray shadows between the moonbeams and tapped from the ledges in the map hidden between the contour lines.

I had to go. I could not explain. The answer would be at the other end of the journey. I knew I would not return. The journey would bring profound changes. I never questioned it.

"It's out there—somewhere—and I am missing it."

*Somewhere—in Canyonlands*

# 2. Away—But Not Yet Gone

**The bike ride—Day 3 (mid day):**

According to doctrine attributed to Aristotle, Nature abhors a vacuum.

There is more than one kind of vacuum. One type results by removing everything possible from a volume of space. Another type results from monotony. I'm not sure what Aristotle had in mind, but my nature seems to especially abhor the second type of vacuum. My life was not boring, but a certain repetition had set in that was starting to leave me empty. Riding my bicycle broke the monotony when I was a kid. Maybe it would work again.

My journey began with a gigantic one-way-leap airline flight from Austin to Salt Lake City. I spent most of the flight with my nose pressed against the window, watching the progression of landforms slipping beneath the wing. I imagined the view to which I was privileged was commissioned with the wealth of an ancient king who died before its realization. The most profound thinkers in his kingdom hypothesized the existence of the view of the world from above. Once the king learned about the theory of aerial view, he became obsessed by the quest to obtain it.

I connected dots—hills to valley, valley to river, river to dry washes, dry washes to plateaus, plateaus to canyons. I charted the hives of cities and towns, and the thin ribbons of asphalt that connected them, and also the empty lanes of neighborhoods in the making. My eyes plowed the furrowed fields of cultivated green besieged by vast armies of barren browns and blacks and reds. Hovering just above some of the islands of green were tiny rainbows trailing from irrigating geysers. Here and there were puny reservoirs that fed the geysers, pools collected within narrow crannies and shallow depressions of the rumpled, dry skin of the earth. I imagined an insightful king would have realized his dominion to be a fragile bargain struck upon a wizard's illusion.

According to the Second Law of Thermodynamics, hot inexorably flows towards cold, taking from the hot and adding to the cold until, inevitably, everything that exists is forever locked at the same temperature. The bulldozing of hot towards cold levels more than just the temperature of all things; it levels potential—the potential to do and the potential to create. The leveling also shuffles order into disorder.

While local variances to the Second Law can be temporarily contrived, eventually the Law will irreversibly have its way—everywhere. The universe will in the end succumb to "heat death," so announced the German physicist Hermann von Helmholtz in 1854.

So, the kingdom is doomed and the wastelands will deepen. Most of what appears substantial, even what a king can build, is little more than a stroke of the wizard's wand and will not endure. What is accomplished? There is not just one human outlook, but humans characteristically find purpose in the face of the inevitable. Had the king won his aerial view, would he have seen gardens to defend or wilderness to conquer? Would he have instilled a sense of purpose in his people, or would he have declared that no meaning can reside in what cannot last? Having purpose may fall short of finding meaning, but it brings a sense of peace.

In the distance, I could see the curving silhouette of Earth enveloped by the thin fuzz of brilliant blue atmosphere, fading to the darkness of space only a few dozen miles above me, but veiled from our daily consciousness. Like the edges of the king's gardens stolen from the wilderness, the immensity of space is not far away, just hidden from view. The view from the plane is both beautiful and sobering, worth a king's fortune, but mostly ignored, seldom understood. Perhaps if one stared out the window long enough, a meaning would be delicately implied.

I strained to gain an angle westward, gauging the horizon for the first view of the mountains, wanting to swap the sweeping monotony of the high plains for the crowded confusion of mountains and canyons. Then they were there. Like a mariner of old peering from the crow's nest atop the main mast, within me a voice shouted "Land ho!"

The plane made a quick stop in Colorado Springs. Then it was off again, angling over the parallel ridges of the Rocky Mountains as it pushed for more altitude. The view broadened, and I soaked in the grand sweep of the serrated landscape, trying to identify sets of peaks and scattered towns. The constant parade of mountains tailed off into isolated ranges, high mesas, and wide desert basins. I knew we had reached the western slope of the Rockies and were entering Utah. I looked for areas in which I anticipated riding. One very long, straight ridge with a wavy top caught my attention. "What is that?"

*A mysterious ridgeline somewhere in Southeastern Utah—*
*spied from the plane*

I am uncertain why I am leaving Austin, not to return. I need simplification. Perhaps I have too many gardens to defend or need a new wilderness to explore? The trails, rivers, and lakes around Austin have grown too familiar. The streets, buildings and events of the city are too familiar, as well. And I have grown too predictable in this setting. My relationships are walled-in and pacing about in the cell of repetition. All of this predictability is tedious, not simple.

With the sophistication of a cleaver, I have simplified and streamlined. I've handed all of my responsibilities to my shadow. I've said goodbyes instead of see-you-laters. Besides the stuff I carried onto the plane, I have reduced all that I own to the volume of just six boxes totaling about twelve cubic feet to be sent to me later. I have no expectations and have made no promises. Anything is a possibility. Riding will be my purpose. I will look for meaning somewhere along the road. I have not yet charted my losses.

However lightened, my load includes a hidden mass. Disappointments are stuffed into the crevices and folds of my gear. I haven't exactly failed, but I haven't exactly succeeded, either. My old purposes have faded; new ones have eluded me.

The last few years, I taught math at Austin High School and at the community college. I taught concepts and problem solving, but I also wanted to expose my students to the mystery that enveloped them—the mystery hidden in the patterns of existence. I never got to that chapter even though I tried.

Deep mystery dwells in the power of the terse language of mathematics, especially geometry, to describe the universe. The universe and geometric logic are seemingly inseparable, almost like geometry is the ultimate building material of the universe. Some would dismiss this notion by saying there is no mystery at all, that geometry is a human invention created to mimic the very different reality of existence. But I think that the relationship is much closer. Geometry is discovered, not invented. Only the symbols and expressions of geometry are human inventions. Clues are embedded in the existence that shapes us every day.

The gently curving world I see through the airplane window strengthens the intuitive connection I sense between geometry and the mystery of existence. Perhaps I don't understand the mystery well enough to expose it to others. I want to learn more.

Then the sounds of the jet diminished, and within a few minutes, I felt a tugging in my ears. When the plane turned, I could see the Great Salt Lake in the distance, then the large open-pit copper mine. We were coming down.

Aristotle's doctrine that Nature abhors a vacuum was partially based upon the ferocity with which Nature tries to fill a vacuum. An example (but not one likely known by Aristotle) is the crash of air into the vacuum opened up by lightning, creating thunder. Aristotle took the ferocious filling of vacuums as evidence that Nature avoids making them. But this is not true. While it is true that vacuums do not exist in absolute terms, Nature makes near vacuums in great abundance.

Making vacuums is part of the creative process. A vacuum is a place to be creatively filled. Perhaps this constructive principle also applies to my personal vacuum.

Helmholtz's dreary conclusion about the Second Law of Thermodynamics likewise misses part of the scheme of things. The Second Law demands that there is constant flow—flow of energy and time. The grand flow around us motivates creative processes. Flows and vacuums are intertwined and work together in creation. Both are connected to the mystery of geometry, the mystery from which our world is built and the missing chapter I never got to talk about with my math students.

The plane landed, and I slowly settled down to Earth. The reality of my ride was yet to come. I was far from home, and I had no return ticket. Indeed, I was not really sure I had a home, anymore. I aimed for Santa Barbara, but I didn't know anyone there. In fact, I had never been there except for driving through on US Route 101. And I didn't know what I would do when I finally rode into Santa Barbara. I had not sketched a plan beyond riding, and my plan for riding was only loosely formed. For the moment, I concentrated on getting the ride started.

When I retrieved my bike from the airline, I discovered it had been damaged during the transit. The derailleur side of the rear axle had endured a hard blow. I made adjustments to get it back into working order, after a fashion. But the airline inflicted some damage that couldn't be rectified with my small collection of hand tools. The adjustments devoured the afternoon, and so I abandoned the airport much later than I intended.

I rode against a stiff headwind and in heavy traffic around Salt Lake City. The delay pushed my escape from the city almost into rush hour. Apparently none of these rush hour drivers had ever seen a bicyclist, or at least they didn't recognize that a bike needed a few extra inches of shoulder. Okay, it was I who was out of place. I wanted to pull the ripcord and bail from the city.

Two flat tires interrupted the ride that afternoon and evening. I also needed to stop frequently to make additional adjustments to my battered bike. Most seriously, damage to the derailleur attachment caused the chain to drop onto the spokes the first time I shifted to the lowest gear. I was going nowhere slowly.

The wind settled around dark, so I continued to ride until about midnight. I struggled to get away from populated areas and find a place to camp. I lagged many miles short of where I hoped to be, and I smashed my thumb working on the bike in the dark. My generator-powered head and tail lights blinked out whenever I came to a halt, rendering me precariously invisible. At one busy and unlighted four-way stop, I was certain I would be hit. I wasn't hit, but I was honked at—twice. I taunted myself, "This isn't what I imagined."

Finally, I laid the bike down, pitched my tent in the weeds, and went to sleep in a shallow ditch along an empty stretch of road. I could have easily given up that very first night.

The next morning I discovered the airline had bent the rear axle and a dropout on the frame of my bike. The bent frame element had been responsible for the chain falling onto the spokes the first day. The extensive damage meant backtracking into populated areas for repairs. During the night, the wind had reversed direction to the north and then continued to blow hard. So, once more I pushed against the current, but this time it was a cold current. And it became a wet current as rain riveted me into a bent-over, defensive posture. My knees hurt from pressing so hard against the crisp, chapping wind. Snow painted the tops of the surrounding mountains. But the worst part was that I was headed backwards.

I found a Schwinn shop in Orem, perhaps not a *real* bike shop but the closest thing that I was likely to find in Utah. The young men in the shop were quite helpful and very interested in both my custom touring bike and my trip. They did find an axle among their stock that would fit my bike, not exactly a replacement, but one that would do the job with a little encouragement from a hacksaw and a grinder. I was thankful they were willing to search for a solution rather than just saying, "We don't have one of those."

My sagging spirit was lifted by the fact that my bike was now working reasonably well and by the cheerfulness of the guys at the bike shop. But I remained a little discouraged because it continued to rain intermittently. I was very tired, and my knees were still tender. And I had pedaled about eighty miles without really getting anywhere. I decided to go no further. I needed time to rest and collect myself. I checked into a motel room, took a long hot shower, trued the wheels on my bike, organized my gear, and bought a warm meal at a fast-food restaurant. As I sat and ate by myself, I stared at a big window from the bottom of a trance—one moment, caught in the reflections of the interior; the next moment, lost in the blackness on the other side of the glass. I may have been simplified and streamlined, but the moment felt complicated and confusing. What was I really doing here?

The question faded with sleep.

The next morning dawned clear and cool. By the time I showered again, repaired the two punctured tubes, and bought some provisions, the clock nudged 11:00 A.M. But, at last, I rolled out of town.

To this point, I had been too busy solving problems to be caught by excitement over where I was and what I was attempting. I lost the big picture in the details of bicycle parts and dodging cars. Although surrounded by mountains that wore a shroud of fresh snow in mid-August, the city environment here did not feel much different than the confines of Austin. I was still captive: not yet free to think or miss anyone.

As I rode out of Orem, I passed two kids who were walking along the road. One yelled, "Where are you going?" I felt a sudden jolt of emotional electricity when I shouted back, "California!" I was finally on the loose.

As the snow-dusted peaks around Salt Lake shrank behind me, other mountains poked up in front of me. City things gave way to farms and small towns. Busy commuter routes yielded to little blacktop roads without stripes, used by tractors to hop from field to field. I stopped at a small drive-up (or, in my case, ride-up) diner and filled a canteen with icy soda. I leaned my bike against a pole between the cars and pickups. The contrast had an edge to it. People stared. I felt unordinary. I was uncoiling.

A few hours into my escape, as I braked at a rural road junction, I saw another rider approaching from the right. He would arrive at the junction slightly after I did, so I paused and waited momentarily. I saw that his bike was also loaded, but not as heavily as my own. He grew long, dark, curly hair and a beard to match, and he wore a brown, broad-rimmed hat that barely managed to extend beyond his thick corona of hair. His bike looked scrounged from a garage sale.

As he pulled to the intersection, the first thing he said, without hesitation and before I said anything, was, "Are you Mormon?"

A little shocked, I simply responded, "No."

"Well, you ought to be," was his matter-of-fact reply.

He never introduced himself but did ask where I was headed. When I said, "California," he politely leaked out a feeble, "Oh." But when I added that I was first headed to Capitol Reef, he said, "Oh, that's a good place!"

He was just out for a two-day ride in the area. He lived nearby and liked to take little bike tours close to home. Was it mystery or celebration that made him ride? I don't think he was looking for answers or redemption on his bike. Maybe he was mostly searching for wayward souls to point down the right road. Having purpose is having peace.

Our paths only overlapped for a few miles. We rode together but talked very little. Then he turned one way, and I turned the other. In parting, he did not say goodbye: only that I should think about becoming Mormon.

The day was good for biking. I felt very strong and could have gone farther than I did. Nonetheless, today's ride was my longest ever. Something was trailing me, though—something in the back of my mind that I couldn't yet identify—something that made me uneasy.

During one anxious moment at dusk, I ran over a small snake. I was going too fast and could not dodge it on my heavily laden bike. When I looked back, the snake appeared unhurt and in a hurry.

I slept alongside Highway 28, just outside Gunnison. This was not my plan. I intended to sleep at Yuban State Park but never saw the turn for it. How could I miss a turn while traveling by bicycle? Does the place exist? Was I distracted or lost in thought?

Just before bedding down in my tiny one-person tent, I heard coyotes nearby. So, just to set things straight with them about where they were to be and where I would be, I walked towards them and growled loudly.

Day 1 – 38.9 miles; Day 2 – 37.7 miles; Day 3 – 87.8 miles

# 3. Dreams with Spokes

## Day 4:

Santa delivered my first bicycle when I was five—the kind of bike with solid rubber tires and training wheels. The training wheels were off before the end of the first day. In a childhood that was mostly leaden, riding my bike granted slivers of a chance to be a kid.

I awoke forty-five minutes before sunrise, uneaten by coyotes. I reached for my mental "Start" button, but I felt some resistance. Okay, I definitely wanted to evacuate my impromptu encampment, but getting underway comes with nagging tasks. I pushed against the inertia of the night and the friction of the start.

With the repairs on Day 2 and some subsequent tuning, my bike was adjusted for the ride. Now, I needed tuning. Getting up was not like rolling out of bed. I would have to invent a new routine.

On the bike, my equipment and supplies were streamlined and maximally organized. Pitched, unfurled, and arrayed, the elements of my campsite were orderly and manageable. Transitioning from one configuration to the other amounted to barely corralled chaos, especially at an improvised campsite like this one. There was no way to stand my bicycle erect. There was no table on which to lay things, account for them, and sequence them for storage. There was high grass in which to lose things and dirt to fowl things. And there was no comfortable spot to sit and collect my thoughts into a mental checklist. My stuff rode well on the bike and sheltered me well during the night. I just needed to devise a good way to get from configuration A to configuration B, and back to A again.

I worked against the Second Law, which always tries to change order into disorder. Going from one ordered state to a different ordered state is simply not natural. Kids know this. Adults have to learn. Oh heck, defying the rules of the universe is kind of fun once you get the hang of it!

In my head, I ran through the permutations of how things would come apart or go together. I imagined which things to tuck and roll first, then next, and next. I considered the spaces to be filled, mapping different stuff to places in the bags and on the rack. I mentally charted what I needed to use and when. I created a sequence that would leave nothing behind or out of place. I would remove the bags from my bike, pack them, and then slide them back into place. Except for the tent bag and the sleeping bag stuff sack, no gear would have to touch the ground. Everything would go directly back to its special place. The tent and sleeping bag would have to be strapped onto the rack after the panniers were in place, however. Okay, it wasn't quite a perfect system. The two exceptions to my perfect sequencing bothered me a little, but the system was good, overall.

More and more, I was streamlining procedures to match the sleekness of my gear. I was becoming simpler and more self-contained. I was discovering power and efficiency in my simple, self-contained technologies. As I worked out the kinks, it almost seemed that I could ride forever.

The morning was cold. The cozy warmth of the sleeping bag leaked out of me while packing and loading. Second Law. All of my parts didn't want to operate in the chill. The pistons in my legs didn't quite fit the grooves. The bearings in my knees snagged and dragged. The machinery needed steam from the boiler and the warm touch of sunlight. A little determination would be required to cheat the Second Law.

I cast off by walking rather than riding. When I finally mounted the bike a half-hour after sunrise, my knees quickly became sore from working in the cold air. I rode slowly in a low gear. The day warmed. The boiler heated. The pistons, grooves and bearings fell into place. The soreness evaporated. The Second Law was temporarily defied by working through the problem.

I left busy Highway 89 for the solitude of Utah Highway 24, covering thirty-three miles before stopping for lunch. The day sizzled by lunch, so sultry it was hard to believe that it had been so cold just a few hours earlier. Fortunately, I discovered the shade of some cottonwoods that hugged a small, cool stream and made a fine place to dine. It was a secret improvised waypoint, down the mountainside from the roadway, heard before seen—a world lost to passing motorists but found by me.

Back on the highway after lunch, brief descents occasionally interrupted the long, intense climb. However infrequent, the downhill glides were exhilarating, despite my concern over the loss of hard won elevation. I was trading sweat for adrenalin. On a longer descent, I surfed upon the moment—slipping over the silken roadway with no cars in sight, surrounded by painted mountains and rushing towards the next horizon with mercurial abandon. I was roaming free on planet Utah.

I fixed two more flats just before dark, but I made it to a nice roadside park with water prior to sunset. The roadside park was high along the incline I had battled for much of the afternoon. I was now rewarded with a commanding view of the valley below and the long ridges above. I sat on the top of the table, feet on the bench and sawed lazily at a sandwich as I watched the blues and reds of twilight diffuse into a pink afterglow, faraway beyond the peaks. The wind calmed, and so did I. This was a big place, and I was alone within it. I could not turn a key and flip a switch, and then race through the gathering night until reaching the next town. I was where I was going to be until the dawn.

With the technology of a table available, I abbreviated my simple system even more. I parked my bike upright at the end of the table, inflated my air mattress, and fluffed my down sleeping bag. The table became my bed with a view, a view that quickly faded into unreachable dreams.

I awoke during the night, sometime after moonset. The Milky Way around Cygnus was, in this distant place, still unspoiled by the debris of a crowded world.

Total mileage for the day: 51.1

## Day 5:

*Crossing the first of many high summits*

On the bike and over the top: I spent the morning pedaling uphill, crossing the summit at 8,345 feet. I paused to celebrate reaching my first high summit of the trip, dismounting from my bike and leaning it against the square wooden post that held the summit sign. A small inscription was freshly scratched into the post. Two bicyclists making a coast-to-coast trip carved it when they traversed the summit in the opposite direction a month earlier. The long descent beyond the crest took me through Loa and into Capitol Reef National Park. In Loa, I bought provisions and cold orange juice.

*Colorful but barren cliffs on the road to Capitol Reef*

During the ride up and over my first high summit, I began discovering what would become a persistent reality: the wind blows a lot in the Southwest and most often it is aimed against or across my path. Not only did I have to work against the double whammy of gravity and wind on the uphill, but the gale sometimes blew so hard on the downhill side of the mountain that I had to pedal to generate any forward motion. Gravity borrows and returns in predictable cycles, but the wind mostly takes according to whim and seldom returns more than a tease.

Dwelling upon the accounting of the pushes and pulls of the ride would only make the ride unbearable. I wasn't here seeking equity; I was looking for balance of a different sort. Against the bump of the breeze, my mind pushed me from behind. Through a mental snowstorm, I could see the time and place where my ride actually began . . .

When I was a kid back in Texas, I escaped into recurring fantasy about heading west on my bike and not stopping until I ran out of road. I stood along the edge of U.S. 80 looking to the sunset and saw the lines of the highway converge towards the horizon. The horizon in Arlington was unremarkable—low and barely rolling. But I twirled a kaleidoscope vision of distance inside me. I knew that U.S. 80 sliced deserts and mountains, and stretched all the way to California. I imagined mountains. I imagined canyons. I imagined ocean. "Los Angeles," I whispered, "the shores of the Pacific—what places those must be."

Although the seed for this odyssey was planted somewhere in my childhood dreams, the germination only began during the past winter. It started as a migration of mind alone, lacking the structure of an actual plan for a bike trip. It sprouted as a yearning to be somewhere else—a quick fusion of past adventures and past disappointments with the present void in my life; a flash of delirium within the dull ache of wondering if I could break from my routine.

The idea of journeying by bicycle was an evolution so subtle I sometimes don't believe I'm traveling on one. I certainly didn't consider myself to be a serious bicyclist, and I certainly would not have leaped directly to the concept of taking an extended bicycle tour. During the past year, while commuting to my teaching job on a bicycle, I was impressed with both the simplicity and efficiency of bike travel. I was cycling "around town" a lot, often thirty to forty miles in a day. Gradually, I began to consider what it would be like to straighten these thirty to forty mile rides into a single direction, putting several of them end to end. Then, one day, the restlessness that was barely contained within me mated with my curiosity about bicycle travel. In a what-the-heck-I've-got-nothing-better-to-do moment, the trip was born. The bike is my vehicle but not one I have yet grown accustomed to carrying me so far.

As I convert the symbols and lines on my map into places seen from the saddle of my two-wheeled stick-pony, the bike is becoming an integral part of the experience—almost an extension of my being and the rod by which I measure my daily reality. Gravity is metered by its gearing, as are the winds. Time is counted out by the cadence of the pedals. Space is measured by the winding of the little odometer attached to the front wheel. Life's burdens must fit within the panniers and handlebar bag. Fate is the next gray-line road on the map. Direction is the needle on the compass. Getting a grip on a situation is squeezing the brake levers just enough to stop or slow without heating the air in the inner tubes enough to blow a tire.

Connections are becoming simple and direct. The forces of nature are being welded to my subconscious processes. Reality is sorted into miles and elevation rather than by schedules and calendars.

Traveling on a bicycle is fun! The physical effort stirs my inner chemistry. Feelings are amplified. Senses are sharpened. Reality is changing. The elegance of this new reality is beginning to capture me. It's more than I anticipated.

But something is nagging me; I still don't know what it is.

Enjoying a challenge and having fun are not really the same. One is serious and calculated, while the other is light and spontaneous. On rare occasions the two can merge. I have had a few such moments so far, vivid moments of uncanny energy and awareness. Mostly I am enjoying the challenge while I adjust to a new reality or see old ones with fresh eyes. But something unknown is stalking me.

I have discovered another persistent reality: traveling alone over large, desolate expanses can be a lonely experience. The loneliness sparks a longing to share the elegance of a difficult task accomplished by simple means—with a woman. Okay, my chemistry *is* stirred up by all my physical activity. But what woman would consider such an insane adventure as this one?

I am sometimes surprised by my own strength and energy, but I am also occasionally reminded of my human exposures despite my propensity to deny them. It is already apparent that the elements of this trip are working like a magnifier, stretching and intensifying both my strengths and frailties. Is this the greatest danger ahead of me?

My solitude is broken here and there by the kindness of strangers. Most people are good to me and interested in my voyage. I believe there is child-like dimension in people that mostly lies dormant. An encounter with a crazy guy on a bike in darn near the middle of nowhere, challenging himself and nature in such a simple manner, seems to liberate the dormant child in the people I meet, at least for a few wistful moments. Some folks ask me questions as if they are starting their own bicycle trip tomorrow, and then they climb back into their motorhomes and drive towards Lake Powell. I've chatted with a number of retirees on extended escapes. Many have bikes lashed to the back of their motorhomes. Mostly, they use the bikes to get around campgrounds, but I can tell from the questions they ask that many of them still like to dream young.

I coasted to a stop in front of the visitor center at Capitol Reef National Park in mid-afternoon. The day turned a bit cloudy, providing some welcome relief as I completed the ride. The tide of kindness from strangers continued to rise when the rangers declared that someone who had biked so far must camp for free.

I rode the short distance to the campground and selected a site. I leaned my bike against the end of the picnic table and then pitched my one-person tent. I stretched my sleeping bag and air mattress inside. I spread provisions over the table and foraged for my dinner among them. I assembled a sandwich and opened a bag of dried fruit, setting aside a can of dessert for later. For a better view of the campground and the surrounding cliffs, I sat on the top of the table with my feet resting on the bench.

This is my first real campsite, and I am clearly enjoying it. The amenities and security of the campground feel quite luxurious to me. But I am feeling something else, too—a sense of disbelief that I actually made it here, all the way from Salt Lake City on a bicycle. I also feel a bit of vulnerability about being in a remote setting with only a bike to carry me home—wherever home really is, now.

Not far up the campground loop is a site harboring two large, identical motorhomes and two jeeps that were towed here behind the motorhomes. I dub this site "nesting motorhomes with offspring." The contrast between my little campsite and the one with the nesting pair of motorhomes underscores my sense of displacement. But it also strengthens my child-like fascination with making this experiment work. I can visualize myself being eight-years old again, standing at the edge of old US Route 80 wondering if I can see any mountains by staring hard enough into the sunset, where its blacktop lanes converge.

*First stop in a campground—in Capitol Reef*

The campground is green and shady, garden like, in fact. Embedded in an old orchard created by early Mormon settlers, the garden is a living remain of the village they called Fruita. The orchard is irrigated by tapping the nearby Fremont River. The garden setting in which I am happily perched, for the moment, certainly stands in bizarre contrast to the barren cliffs that ring it.

I finish my feast, and tire of idle musings and sitting still. I return to the visitor center for a while and look at the old schoolhouse. What would it have been like to go to school in this one-room schoolhouse? Would the rimming canyon walls and tiny schoolhouse create a sense of isolation, like a group of kids stranded in a lifeboat waiting for rescue, listening to repetitive stories to pass the hours? Did the students sometimes hike to the highest viewpoint to discuss the grand sweep of the rumpled terrain and talk about the wonders crouching beyond the horizon in various directions? Was this school beyond the reach of new ideas and discoveries, or did new ideas dance spontaneously amid the mixed chatter of this shoebox schoolhouse?

I am trying to be in that time rather than looking backward to that time. It's not easy to imagine "then" without the prejudices of "now." What is more mystifying: to look at the world when essentially *every-thing* is a mystery but the true complexities are not suspected—or to look at the world when the complicated workings are more appreciated but the underlying reasons are still not understood?

I imagine a map hanging from one wall of the classroom. What did it show? Perhaps my imagination is tilted hopelessly askew by my exposure to modern maps, but when I see old maps my reaction is that things look obviously odd. Proportions look strained. Rivers are too short to feed lakes that look too big, and river basins don't drain enough area to account for the flows. Also, the interior features of the continents appear too large for coastal contours. And, of course, there are the blank spots in old maps, hidden in the haze of rumor and legend.

I like to think, if these were the maps of my childhood, the blank spots and odd shapes would have called to me, and I would have gone off to draw a new map or two.

Before sunset, I take a short hike along the Fremont River and then return to camp. Around the tabletop in my luxury-suite campsite, the day dissolves into darkness. I play with my long shadows thrown down by the lanterns dotting the campground. I brush my teeth. I stow my gear for the night and scoot backwards into my little tent. Already, solitude is the heaviest load I carry.

Total mileage for the day: 45.5

## Day 6:

My eyes blink open with the sky already turning from gray to blue but with no sunlight yet varnishing the sides of the nearby mountains. Today is a hiking day, no biking at all. The targeted hike extends from the campground to the high point on the Frying Pan Trail. The campground is at an elevation of about 5,400 feet, and my turn-around at Lookout Point will be above 6,400 feet.

*Molly's Nipple and tilted layers of rock along the Waterpocket Fold*

Capitol Reef is a land of soft rock and hard elements. The countless thrusts of nature's tiny swords have whittled deep wounds into the rainbow entrails of the land. But many of the same elements have made, with a little help from man in some cases, the very softest parts of the land green and fertile.

The earth here is not just dissected; it is sculpted. The complexity of form is as if the rock were suddenly poured from the sky and frozen in place at mid-splash. The enormous foundations of the convoluted crests tilt upward into great, rusted plunges. The long, rutted cliffs sometimes stretch to the horizon. While the valleys and hillsides are liberally (at least for a desert) covered with vegetation, the immense cliffs are scrubbed barren. In this place, the outer limits of visible life are clearly defined.

Capitol Reef is a focal point for the staggering sweep of geologic time and the crushing forces buried in the earth. The intensity of The Reef stems from its piggy-back ride along the spine of a hundred-mile long crease in the earth, called the Waterpocket Fold, that was pinched upward as the immense and lofty Colorado Plateau was heaved into the sky, far beyond the horizon to the east.

Wherever great cliffs are seen, huge amounts of time are exposed. The eroded flanks of The Reef bare a lengthy cross-section of Earth's history dating backward to the Permian Period, 250 million years into the dimness of the past. But Capitol Reef is unusual in that time is stretched across its horizontal floors as well as its vertical walls. This is because of its position on the crest of the great fold. As the layers of rock were buckled and bent upward over the past ten million years, the folded edges have been clawed away by the erosive forces of the earth—first, along a narrow line in the youngest and topmost layers of rock, then spreading outward east and west away from the axis of the fold as the bending and thrusting continued—ever wider in space and ever deeper in time. The tilted edges of the rock layers jut above the fringing valleys because the upward thrust slightly out-paces the downward carving. The oldest formations straddle the center of the fold, with the very oldest rocks bleeding through the incisions at the bottoms of the canyons, near the centerline of the eroded kink.

*Eroded faces of tilted rock layers exposed across the*
*valley paralleling the ridgeline of the Waterpocket fold*

In many places around the park, the folding, thrusting and gnawing of the rock that have occurred are strikingly apparent. Both the linear ridges and the intervening terraced valleys are marked with colorful bands that indicate the long march of geologic time. The ridges slope modestly to one side, conforming to the angle of the fold, but cascade sharply away on the other side, where the upward tilting layers have been chewed off by erosion. The striated valleys, typically bordered by cliffs on one side and slopes on the other side, are plowed into parallel channels along the exposed ends of softer rocks that have been more aggressively whittled away by the elements. The ticks of time are more obviously displayed in the striped faces of the cliffs, but the subtly ribbed valleys are even more remarkable since geologic time is not usually stretched along the horizontal surfaces of the land.

The top of the trail arrives quickly, three and a half miles in just over an hour. Some rain clouds meander overhead, occasionally thumping out a half-hearted drumbeat of thunder. A light sprinkle teases but does not quench. There is no real threat, and I have plenty of time to linger on the summit.

The vista from this high perch demands inspection. I'm sure that I can see at least seventy-five miles in some directions. Off just north of east, slashes of canyons crisscross a high plateau. This is in the general direction of Canyonlands, a realm crouching within my near future. I strain to see the transitions from here to there. I can distinguish the forms of dissected mesas and see pinkish-red hues reminiscent of Canyonlands and its outer perimeter. But the curvature of the earth, the northern slopes of the Henry Mountains, and the intervening plateaus hide the features of Canyonlands from my line of sight. In my mind's eye only, I see the spires and buttes, the prominent gorges, and the broad basins of Canyonlands. I know they are out there. My compass points the direction.

I also look towards the southeast, in the direction of Lake Powell, another place in my future. The high ground near the lake combines with the deep depression in which the lake sits to conceal it from view. I imagine my route from here to there. It's a long way.

The sightlines are pulled taut by the expanses. I sense magic in the multiplication that my bicycle performs—multiplying the turns of my feet into distances too far to see their other ends. My bike looks so modest. Would anyone else see the Multiplication Magician hidden in the tubes, sprockets and spokes? I am reminded of seeing one of John Wesley Powell's old dories used to explore the Green and Colorado rivers. Looking at it didn't convey the distances covered and the adventures created in it.

The future fades into the hazy distance and the uncertainty of events yet to be. For the moment, I will ride my daydream.

# 4. Through the Reef—and into the Open

**Day 7:**

On the eve of my departure from Austin, my good friends in the local Sierra Club tossed a party to say goodbye. For the finale of the festivities, my friends awarded various ceremonial titles to individuals in the group. Mine was the last title announced: most intrepid. Stumbling for words and resisting tears, I responded, "I'm not the intrepid one—my bike is." And so, my bike became *Intrepid*.

Today was Sunday. The day of the week was getting harder to calculate. Had I not overheard a conversation about it, I'm certain I would not have known or cared. Not only have I ridden into my own time zone, but I have also scratched my own calendar.

In the early morning, I rode uphill to the Goosenecks, a deep, twisting, steep-walled canyon carved by Sulphur Creek. Cottonwoods line this perennial stream, making its grass-covered banks a true oasis, one that is inaccessible from my vantage point on the plateau above. I could see two hikers walking the trail at the bottom of the canyon. Should I take a day to explore Sulphur Creek from below? I would like to hike the trail, but the urge to move on may be too strong to overcome.

The steep climb to the Goosenecks Overlook folded back four miles in the direction from which I entered the park. As a section of a journey that started in one place and will end in another, backtracking seemed awkward. But the view was worth it. Why did I not stop here on the way into the park? I don't know; I had plenty of time. Perhaps some sense of urgency steered me past the overlook. I want to learn to pause as I make my way.

The downhill return ride was fast and easy, just as it was the first time I did it. With much of my gear stowed in my pitched tent, I allowed my downhill speed to build higher than I normally would. Wheeeeeeeeeeeee. Okay, that must have been the reason I backtracked!

When I got back to camp, I packed lunch and dinner and hiked to the Fremont River overlook. I planned to stay on this ridge to watch the sunset but was chased down by an intense thunderstorm, ripped by searing bolts of lightening. I flew down the trail, making it to my campsite just before the storm cut loose. During the tempest, I

huddled in my little one-person tent along with much of my gear,
listening to the echoes of thunder rumble in long refrains along the
cliffs. In the span of approximately half an hour, the sky poured about
one inch of water onto The Reef before breaking into a brilliant orange
glow. A rainbow hovered beneath the cliffs, right in the valley. And a
double rainbow arched above the precipices while the faces of cliffs
teared with cascading waterfalls.

Although I missed the sunset, Earth had just delivered a spectacular physics demonstration. Adrift on an intrepid bike with an
armful of gear, I realized I am part of this physics experiment because I
am so exposed.

I am not certain there is a purpose to my journey. If someone were
to ask me, "Why are you making this trip?" I would be stymied for an
answer. My intuition tells me it is personal experiment connected to
finding purpose for my version of life. Life may not carry a universal
purpose, much less a universal meaning; yet there are some constants.
Perhaps the closest thing to a universal purpose is to turn the crank
and go forward, letting each individual harvest their own purpose along
the way. Maybe all that exists will someday collapse into a lightening
bolt that just disappears without the roll of thunder being left behind
and without anyone left to hear it. Would the purpose be lost? If the
world ended today, this isolated piece of it probably wouldn't disappear
until tomorrow.

## Day 8:

I packed my stuff and headed towards Lake Powell and Natural
Bridges National Monument. Today would be busy, crammed with
activity from first light to well into the darkness. And it would be a day
of transition from the sanctuary of The Reef to the open, scorched
badlands. Today would also mark the transition from being "a visit" to
"a journey" since I was leaving my first major waypoint and starting to
string a number of waypoints together. And I was beginning to bicycle
across the folds in the map.

I spent more of the morning hiking than biking. I hiked to Hickman
Bridge and partway up Grand Wash before being chased out by another
thunderstorm. The natural bridge is large and stout. I walked beneath
and beyond the natural bridge and looked back to see the rounded,

polished-white butte called Capitol Dome, perhaps a mile distant, framed by the natural bridge.

Capitol Reef derived its name from two sources, one being this rounded dome that reminded settlers of the capitol building. The "reef" part of the name stemmed from the hundred-mile long ridgeline that created a substantial barrier for travelers like a reef does to mariners.

Passages through The Reef (and the greater Waterpocket Fold) were found along canyons cut by the few creeks and rivers that traverse the fold. Ancestral streams were in place before the fold was lifted, and these streams sliced through the buckling rock layers as quickly as they were thrust upward. The Fremont River, fed by Sulphur Creek, cut such a corridor across The Reef, the one now followed by Utah 24.

I was confronting the problem of what to do with my bicycle and gear while hiking. I hauled a lock and cable for the bike itself but had no way of securing my gear. I felt more confident leaving my gear unattended in the campground but did not have a good feeling about leaving it at a trailhead. I decided the best thing I could do was hide my gear away from the trailhead, with or without the bike, depending on the circumstances.

As I rode out of Capitol Reef, I passed a small waterfall spilling into a deep alcove, set back from the road. The morning rains had probably created the fall, but the water was unusually clear for runoff. Without hesitation, I stopped for a shower in the fall. I surprised myself with how relaxed I was about taking the whole morning to explore the trail and enjoy myself, doing things like cooling down in a waterfall—especially since I needed to pedal about eighty miles before the end of the day to avoid setting up another makeshift campsite in the middle of nowhere.

My route along Utah 24 took me around the northern end of the Henry Mountains and provided an excellent view down the length of the range. I stopped at the stores in Caineville and Hanksville, the latter marking the junction with Utah 95. Making stops at isolated country stores has become quite a welcome ritual for me. The outposts render shade and ice-cold drinks, even orange juice, in settings where shade and something cold to drink assume the demeanor of divine interventions. These waystations are much more than gas stations or "convenience stores." They usually combine the attributes of a small grocery store, two-pump gas station, sit-for-awhile rest stop, and community center. The folks running and patronizing these stores tend to be genuinely friendly and inquisitive, even concerned, and they have provided me with welcome relief from my solitude.

Caineville also has a Mexican café that several people told me is very good. Alas, my timing was off. It was closed on Mondays and Tuesdays. Some synchronization is still required with the rest of the world! I stared wistfully at the menu on the window and the empty tables inside. Then I pedaled *Intrepid* on down the road.

Utah 95 is a great highway for bicycling, but I underestimated the solitude one can experience in this vast land. Sometimes, from horizon to terraced horizon, I and the road were the only visible traces of human existence. The horizons were distant ones, too: farther than a day's ride, farther than distinct vision—almost farther than the mind's eye could reach to the next friendly outpost.

Somehow, when I grasped for the comfort of good memories to help fortify me against the isolation, the faces most easily summoned were those that said goodbye under unfortunate circumstances. Such was the un-anchoring of this expanse. My travel did not seem like a vacation but rather like an odyssey. Sirens beckoned me to untangle what-ifs already dashed upon the rocks. Sometimes my mind lingered in Austin, and sometimes it leaped forward to a sunset over the Santa Barbara Channel. I wanted to discover wonders ahead, but first I had to let go of the past.

Except for the late start and the resulting exposure to the mid-day sun, the bicycling this day was rather easy for the most part. Tracking the transitions in the landscape continued to fascinate me: moving from valley to high plateau and then back to valley; nearly circling an entire set of mountains, absorbing the changing perspective; climbing towards a line that truncated the horizon and then falling off the other side of it. To understand the mystery all around, one must revel in the simplest things—like a shift in perspective. An essential element of Einstein's Theory of Relativity is the untangling of changes in physical perspective. Perhaps essential to the understanding of life is the untangling of different human perspectives.

I covered 82.1 miles, doing the last twenty in the full moonlight as I biked into the night. There were many cottonwoods along this last twenty miles or so. Even in the faded light, the trees contrasted starkly with the bare, dark-red sandstone cliffs against which they grew.

As I descended towards Lake Powell along Utah 95, great cliffs rose eerily in the silver moonlight. The night hovered in stillness, and the blanketing background noises of vehicles hissing and howling emptied from the canyon. Nothing mechanical pierced the silent night except for the intermittent clicking of the freewheel on my bike whenever I coasted. Funneled and amplified by the high walls of narrow side canyons, I could hear the shrieks and whines and growls and squeals of night creatures. The scene stood dream-like—a stage with a painted vision of the Triassic or some other lost age. My own motion seemed stolen from the quiet, and I half expected a giant monster from a fretful nightmare to leap from a shadow and devour me. A sudden loud pop from a cooling guardrail startled me, almost knocking me from the saddle.

I arrived at the water's edge long after I could first hear the lazy licking of tiny waves lapping the rocks below me. Facing the moon, the quilted surface of the water alternated in streaks of silver and black. I stuck my hand into the water; it was invisible below the surface. The water was wash-basin warm, but the evaporation afterward was cool and stimulating.

I slept in the open that night, on a high rock by the shore of Lake Powell. The full moon shining on my face made me crazier than I already was, I'm sure. I woke from time to time and sat up to look around. The bedroom quiet invited casual inquiry. Ghostly moonlit silhouettes hid the details and created a world that could be dissected and rear-ranged by the imagination. I saw creatures disguised in the shapes of rocks. I heard faint splashes of very old and gnarly things, hidden by the black surface of the lake. The gentle rain of starlight dissolved the nudge of time so that old things could lurk again. I was certain that I had awakened something prehistoric, and it was watching me from beyond the shore. It's funny how a silly fantasy can catch you for a moment and even speed your heartbeat and shorten your breath. And then you wonder, "What was that about?" I don't think it was monsters that scared me.

At the end of the fantasy, the moonlight did what it always does to me—left me with an unexplained sadness—like it did back in Austin when it spilled over the map upon my wall.

**About my bike:**

My touring bicycle *Intrepid* is not fancy, but after riding 350 miles over varied terrain with a heavy load, I can say it is adequate for the task. Since my bike was assembled from components just a few weeks before my departure and tested very little, I was concerned it might not be up to the task. Moreover, it was tested under conditions far less demanding than the ones I'm encountering on my journey. I guess I could say the same about myself, so my bike and I had something to assert. My bicycle could certainly be improved (also true for me), but it's doing pretty well (and so am I). And it wasn't too expensive (and I'm cheap company for it).

The heart of my bike is a lightweight frame made by an upstart company named Trek, located in Waterloo, Wisconsin. It's a small company that only makes frames, not complete bikes. Judging from the serial number, they had made fewer than one thousand frames when mine was built, probably last year, in '79. The frame looks like a nicely executed imitation of the famous British frames made by Mercian, at a much lower cost. The material is Reynolds 531, just like the Mercian frames, and the geometry is essentially identical. The lugs on the Trek frame are not as fancy as the intricate lugs on the Mercian frame. But it is silver soldered like the Mercian and probably just as strong.

My bike is equipped with a double crank and a six-cog freewheel, making it a twelve-speed bike. Avoiding the two "extreme crossover" positions means that I have ten usable gear ratios. I considered equipping my bike with a triple crank, which would have made it an eighteen-speed bike (sixteen usable speeds). But I opted for the more economical and easier-to-shift double crank, instead.

Having only a limited number of gear ratios available, I chose to emphasize the low and mid gear ranges, while sacrificing the very high gear range. This tradeoff has proven to be very successful. The crank has chain rings with forty-six and thirty-four teeth, and the freewheel carries cogs from fourteen to thirty-four teeth. Thus, my lowest gear is twenty-seven gear-inches (meaning that I travel forward twenty-seven inches for every full turn of the crank), and my highest gear 88.7 gear-inches.

Now that I have done more realistic "testing," I wish I had selected the triple crank. The primary motivation for this change would be to gain one or two gear ratios lower than the twenty-seven gear-inch ratio available to me now. I think a gear ratio as low as twenty-one gear-inches would be desirable. In selecting a triple crank, I would still not include very high gear ratios, probably limiting the top-end to no more than ninety-three gear-inches, while continuing to emphasize low and mid gears. Overall, I think the sixteen usable gear ratios offered by an eighteen-speed bike would be more than adequate for any situation, provided they are chosen properly. In the meantime, I am doing okay with my twelve-speed bike.

Strong wheels are essential. Mine are built from strong, but economical, Weinman concave rims, and thirty-six 14-gauge stainless steel spokes in a four-cross lacing pattern. I am riding on 1.5 inch tires, which are a good compromise between soft-ride, load-carrying capacity, and low rolling resistance.

Although I have good brakes on my bike, this is another area where I wish I had spent a bit more money. Going down the long mountain grades with a heavy load requires a lot of braking to keep speeds at safe levels. A brake set with a greater mechanical advantage would be valuable.

My touring bike is not equipped with sealed bearings, so I must carry tools and parts to service the bearings in the hubs and bottom bracket. Not going with sealed bearings saved money, but I think my next touring bike will have them.

For carrying the load, my bike is equipped with a Blackburn rear rack. It supports two simple, medium-sized panniers, as well as my tent and sleeping bag strapped on top. The rest of my load (mostly my camera gear and a canteen) is carried in a handlebar bag. I made my own water bottle cage for the frame, one that would hold a larger-than-normal one-quart canteen in an insulated cover.

I could have added a front rack and front panniers, but I wanted to keep my load minimized and streamlined. This decision was not so much about weight and aerodynamics as it was about psychology.

Overall, I would characterize my bicycle as good, but nowhere near top-of-the-line. I used predominantly mid-range components bolted to an excellent frame. Were I to choose again, I would mostly follow the same strategy—upgrading to a triple crank, better brakes, and sealed bearing hubs.

*Intrepid*

# 5. Hidden Time

**Day 9:**

Morning always sweeps away the monsters of night and brings new optimism.

I awoke to the sounds of waves lapping the rocky shoreline. I had enough sleeping on a rock! The air mattress helped, as did the sleeping bag I lay on top of most of the night. But the sandstone surface seemed to grow harder during the night, and its frozen contours didn't quite match the ones of my body.

The sun, though still very low to the horizon, blazed with a piercing intensity. The sky shared the same cobalt hue with the deep waters that filled the once mighty canyon. The large rock I sat upon would seem a dizzying lofty perch along the canyon rim were it not for the drowning of the chasm beneath the shimmering surface of the reservoir. I tried to imagine the view before the canyon was dammed. The world before me harbored a few scrawny shadows but was mostly slicked with harsh yellow-white sunlight. The sunken inner gorge would have been steeped in bluish ghost-light. The tumbling chime of canyon wrens would have echoed in directionless serenade. The rumble and gurgle of rapids would have mixed with the cascading notes of the wrens and replaced the monotonous slapping of waves. I would have been looking down, way down, into a hidden secret world. Instead, I looked across the lake's surface to more of the same mostly horizontal sun-baked world in which I sat.

Yes, I conceded that Lake Powell was a beautiful reservoir, and I knew that a lot of houseboats had a very good home here. But I wasn't sure that was enough to make the trade.

I packed quickly and set out towards Natural Bridges, crossing the unnatural one spanning Lake Powell. As I climbed steeply away from the reservoir, I watched the growing panorama of blue water against red rock, surrounded by a basin of creamy yellows and subdued greens and topped by red buttes propped against flawless blue sky, creating a ragged skyline.

Up the highway I crossed a short bridge, the kind that one would fly across in a second when traveling by car. Over the railing I peered downward, my vision tumbling perhaps 500 feet into a sheer-walled gorge barely wider at its top than its floor, the shadowy gravel bed locked away from the searing desert beyond. I was developing an even greater understanding of the treasures that were lost to the world of air when the narrow inner gorge of Marble Canyon was subdued by the flooding of Lake Powell. The flotillas of lazy houseboats puttering about the reservoir's surface belied the yawning chasm that was hidden below. I was almost certain that making a home for houseboats (or making electricity for homes in Los Angeles) was not enough.

The climb to Natural Bridges proved long, hot, and brutal. The air hung with uncanny stillness. When I would pause, the only air movements I could feel were the convection currents rising from the pavement. I drank frequently, but no amount of water seemed enough to cool me. The intensity of the heat lifting from the road surface and the steepness of the grade in some stretches chopped my pace into a drunkard's stagger. The climb totaled about 3,000 feet, but the blast-furnace heat made it feel like more.

I reached Natural Bridges just before dark. The campground was full, but two geology professors from Weber State College, located in Ogden, Utah, saw me circling and looking for a spot. They took me into their campsite, and they even fed me a hot meal—and best of all, plied me with cold orange juice. The two professors were there without students, planning future field trips for their classes. They were obviously practiced in caring for the dazed and confused who had spent too much of the day out in the sun.

Total mileage for the day: 55.0  Total mileage for the trip: 407.4

## Day 10:

I rested in camp, took a canteen shower, wrote a letter and studied the displays at the visitor center. I would normally be on the road or trail early, but I felt unhurried in my morning meanderings. This was odd. Typically, I felt an inner push when I had some place to go or some task to complete, especially if I faced a challenge and uncertain outcome. Yes, and I was unusually settled the morning I left Capitol Reef, too—not feeling the need to push then, either.

The realization suddenly struck me that I had bicycled into my own time zone—responding to an inner rhythm rather than a clock. I was unusually attached to the moment despite being filled with memories and ripe with expectations. I carried a relaxed feeling that I seldom have. I was equipped with no plan, no schedule, and no definite route, yet I was certain I would have enough clarity, time and direction to do what I needed. I shaped each day as it came along, filling it completely.

It is odd how the here-and-now can elude human beings despite the fact our bodies are held firmly within its grip. As my odyssey progressed, I seemed to capture the ability to experience each moment as if it were passing in slow motion. How can time be so elastic yet so rigidly meter our existence? And even as I fill each second with a full sense of the moment, my mind constantly simmers with flashes from the past and visions of the future. It's as if each second is briefly held, and then divided to reveal more seconds hidden within it—scales within time.

Can I maintain this connection with the immediate or will it evaporate in the tedious hours of slowly pushing across the wide landscape?

Late in the afternoon, I struck out to bike the loop that swings near all of the major bridges. I parked my bike to hike to Sipapu and Kachina bridges. The appearance of these bridges from the road did not convey their true size. A more direct experience was needed to affix the scale. As I approached Sipapu, the first bridge to which I hiked, I was concentrating on my feet as I briskly walked the trail, not looking ahead to the bridge. Suddenly, the trail ended. When I looked up, I was startled by the immensity of the bridge arcing high above my head, at least fifty feet up, dividing the ink-blue sky. Scale.

Arriving back to camp just before dark, the friendly professors fed me hot dogs and more orange juice.

*Sipapu Natural Bridge stetching overhead*

**Day 11:**

The clock inside me ticked a bit faster this morning. I launched early to hike to the remaining bridge, Owachomo. To me, this bridge was the prettiest of the three large bridges. It was also the shortest hike.

*The delicate span of Owachomo Natural Bridge*

By the time I returned to camp to get my gear, the two friendly professors, Sid and Don, had departed. However, they left a can of cold orange juice for me. The generosity and thoughtfulness of the two professors from Weber State was astonishing. Perhaps they accumulated their nurturing instinct by teaching in a classroom without walls.

There was no time to linger in appreciation, though. I soon straddled the bike and found the road, again. A sense of purpose urged me onward although I wasn't sure what that purpose was. Maybe it was simply to turn the crank?

Lunch stop landed at the Mule Canyon Anasazi ruins, another waypoint with a terrific view. As I chomped on my sandwich, I thought of the Indians who often ate at this same spot but who did so a thousand years before. Same spot—different time. I paused in the magic of this.

I was staring at the ants that were foraging for crumbs and watching one particular ant that was tugging at a piece more than twice its own size when I was overcome by a very strange thought. I could see parallels between the lives of the Anasazi people that once made this hilltop their home and the lives of the ants that still do. Both gathered food. Both toiled outside. Both made simple shelter using materials splintered from the earth. One was conscious and questioning—one driven by imperatives alone. Both were organized and purposeful, survival being an immediate and un-delegated concern. One gone—one still here. Same spot—different time. Different scale.

The bold and vast view of this hilltop must surely have meant something to the Anasazi who chose it for their home. Their practical connection to nature was as compelling as that of the ant, needing to select a good location for their home in order to survive. But the Anasazi, unlike the ants, also realized the sweep of the earth around them and the flight of stars overhead. The view must have been important, too. They could not see the sun as a star or a day as the turning of Earth. But they probably did sense the mystery and depth of the universe and understood that hidden forces and schemes shape the world and its events. The view linked them to these greater realities even if it did not explain them. Spiritually, they must have been connected to the whole of existence in a way that we have surely lost since we have constructed the illusion of control and separation. Same spot—different time. Different reality.

I never tire of the distant views. Each climb harbors a treasure at its top. And this stretch of road is blessed with wonderful views of the Four Corners region. My mind flashes to a classroom in my grade school years, the teacher pointing on a map to the spot I now see on a different scale. My mind skips from the convergence of pink, purple, green and yellow on that roll-down map to the plateaus and peaks and basins that shrink into the distance before me. I remember being curious about all the places she would poke with her finger. I wonder if she would believe the homework assignment that I am doing.

I am the assignment. I took out my map and compass to check just how far I could see.

Getting on a bike and pedaling as far as I am going teaches that the world is not so big, after all. One place is connected to another, and that place is connected to the next. And there are only so many places in this world. My bike connects the dots. Geography is measured by canteen and sandwich.

The view in the distance is marred by the haze from the coal-fired power plant just beyond the Four Corners. This plant continues to belch huge plumes of smoke from its stacks because it was given exemptions from the Clean Air Act of 1972. Perhaps Congress thought no one would notice in this out of the way place—out of the way, yes, but not beyond the range of a bicycle.

*The jagged backbone of Comb Ridge*

Off to the east, not as high as the horizon, stretches a striking wavy-topped ridge. It seems familiar to me. I search for the recollection. The distances to the east are stacked in layers: the nearby juniper flat; a line of rounded hills beyond; the low wide wash; the wavy ridge; higher plateaus; straight ridges; then mountains; then fuzzier and more distant mountains; and cumulus clouds below empty blue sky. It's not a picture. It's a stage waiting to be entered. Today's ride across this stage projects as a tough one but an interesting one.

I leave the Anasazi ruins and descend into the broad valley crossing Mule Canyon Wash. There I pause at the blunt chin of the chopped-off face of Comb Ridge. What was striking and curious from the highlands behind me now stands imposing and awe provoking.

From my vantage point straddling my bike at the base of the escarpment, Comb Ridge marks the edge of the earth. I look across Highway 95 to the south and see the humping ridgeline plow all the way to the horizon. I look across Highway 95 to the north to see the same unbroken wave of the ridge marching all the way to that horizon. Viewed from the center stripe of the two-lane bridge over the wash, Comb Ridge is the wall where the Earth simply ends. Its white crown shines boldly over the darker greens and rusted browns and reds of the valley, daring anyone or anything to pass. The world may be smaller than I once thought, but this is still a very large ridge—and a tall one to climb over on a bike. Scale—up close scale.

*The world seemed to end at the blunt face of Comb Ridge.*

I could remember seeing Comb Ridge from the airplane that carried me to Salt Lake, and I could remember thinking "That's interesting; I wonder what that is?" It was impressive through the window of the airplane, 35,000 feet above. It's overwhelming from the saddle of a bicycle paused at its foot. Aerial scale versus in-the-middle-of-it scale.

I ride again, following the highway as it is forced to the right by the rising ridge. The road climbs in a steep line across the face. I crawl along in the lowest of my twelve gears, pedaling with the same cadence that I would use when sailing across a valley floor but making far less headway with each turn of the crank. What is gravity, anyway? How can it find me here, a tiny spec within this vastness? Climbing Comb Ridge demands patience. The steep grades seem unending. Just when I think I've topped the last barrier, I discover another one hidden around a curve or a bump in the grade, steeper and longer than the last one.

The experience of winching myself up the precipice deepens my sense of scale—immerses me into the scale. The convoluted ridge I spied from Mule Canyon this morning has now zoomed to gigantic proportions in the course of a few hours. The process of welding the two prominent, yet separated, points together with the burn in my muscles brings some satisfaction to my toil. I can see the highlands from which I set sail this morning. I recall the march to those heights. I record the measure of each summit in the scale of my experience. I am connected once again—first, there to here—and now, here to there.

On the steepest sections, I zigzag across the road to lessen the strain. Passing vehicles are usually spread apart by an hour or more. Except in the occasional set of hairpin turns, I can see and hear approaching vehicles miles away. I use whatever portion of road that attracts my fancy, making up new rules—gravity rules.

I invent ways to extend my patience with the slow climb. The metered pace of my ascent allows me to catalogue the litter along the roadway. Utah is a fairly pristine state, overall, but the locals do seem to enjoy marking their route with empty carcasses of Budweisers. I also begin to take note of fake cattle guards painted across the road. Are the cows around here especially dumb? And why is the picture of any animal on a road sign peppered with bullet holes? I must be dehydrating.

When I finally crest the ridge, I am disappointed to see that the glide down the other side is much shorter and less steep than my climb had been. Climbing Comb Ridge is no big deal, after all. I just climbed up the wrong side!

I rode into Blanding, stopping for a shower and a hamburger. I also needed to fix a flat tire there. An old man traveling by RV insisted on "helping" me with the flat. He said he toted a Schwinn in his motor home and was interested in getting a good lightweight bike. I had tapped his dream lightly on the shoulder.

I continued towards Monticello, tracing the heavily traveled US 191. I was still climbing. The sun sagged low, and the thin, high air chilled rapidly. I cranked into the darkness for half an hour, stopping for the night at Devil's Canyon Campground in the Manti-La Sal National Forest at an elevation of about 7,000 feet. The stars drilled through the trees as I fell asleep on a picnic table, a process that must have taken about two minutes.

Total mileage for the day: 49.9 (but should have been measured in inches!)

Accumulated mileage for the trip: 479

# 6. Encounters

## Day 12:

When you wake up on top of a picnic table, it's natural to ask yourself, "What's next?" Okay, the most natural question to ask is, "How in the hell did I get here?" But I'm getting used to waking up on table tops in the middle of nowhere, so I'll just concentrate on the "what's next" question.

Funny thing about waking up in all of the strange situations where my ride happens to end the evening before, no two days start the same way. I may have found a rhythm, but no day is routine. I could not wake up on the next table down the road if I didn't do something different today than I did yesterday.

Every new day links to some goal or event. Some days have something remarkable built into them, like the Mule Canyon Anasazi Ruin and Comb Ridge. Other days must be assembled from more subtle pieces. But every day has the potential to be something special. Today is mostly about cycling from here to Arches National Park along a busy highway, but there are some interesting elements at hand with which to cobble the day.

The fuzzy predawn light uncovers the features around my starting point. Central and southern Utah is not technically a desert but roasts like one in late summer. The Devil's Canyon Campground hunkers in rising terrain south of 11,360 foot Abajo Peak. Wherever Utah pokes above the 6,500-foot level, give or take a little, the vegetation zone transitions from open juniper and piñon woodland to pine forest. A relatively compact area of high terrain, such as the Abajo Mountains, takes on the character of a forest island in a desert sea. To get the effect, one must consider not only what is close but also what is in the distance. I set the first piece into the assembly of the day.

I left the national forest campground about sunrise. The ride started with a steep uphill climb, followed by a long four-mile descent into Monticello. The pour of frigid morning air ripped tears from my eyes and sawed at my fingers. It was remarkable to have such a cold morning sandwiched between scorching hot days. As briefly uncomfortable as the spray of icy air was, I would remember it with some longing in just a few hours. I fitted another piece into the assembly.

Along the ride into Monticello, I passed over several picturesque canyons with steep white walls that contrasted sharply with the dark green forest that nudged right to the edges of the canyon rims. I felt the canyons as I pedaled over them, splashing through rivers of cool air fed by currents spilling down from the highlands. I also smelled the canyons. The scents of the trees concentrated along them and mixed with the added scents of the streams. And I heard the canyons—the echoing of wren songs and the murmur of the water pushing past rocks. Traveling by car, these canyons would be lost beyond the guard-rails. I tapped the next piece of the assembly into place.

Monticello was still sleeping when I slipped through the little town. I noted all the buildings, taking special notice of the post office. Post offices in little out-of-the-way towns seem magic to me—linking the barely-on-the-map places to cities like Denver, New York, Paris and Rome. Yes, it's kind of remarkable that someone in Rome can get a postcard from Monticello, Utah. It makes Rome a better place!

Little towns have scaled-down features of big cities, but these miniaturized versions can be hard to recognize through eyes that are accustomed to the city. For instance, a fifty-foot wide general store takes on the character of an entire shopping mall. Such a matchbox-sized general store might not draw a single customer in Dallas or Denver. What would be dozens of specialized clothing stores at the mall might be reduced to a single isle at the local general store. An entire hardware store might shrink to two shelf units and a display case. The distillations form an interesting commentary, sorting the solid things of everyday life from the frivolous fill-ins.

Certainly, the folks of little Monticello must cart home a few things from Salt Lake City every now and then—or even order an item or two from Denver or Chicago out of a catalog. But the really important stuff is available close at hand, tucked into a corner of some business that stocks hundreds of completely unrelated things instead of many variations of mostly the same thing. There are items that one cannot get in a town like Monticello, but the point is about what you can get, from glazed donuts or a cold beer to a new pair of boots or a radiator cap for your car. Satisfaction sifts from the sorting and the distillation. And what you can't get in town—well, perhaps, you didn't really need it today, anyway.

Monticello to Moab stretched into a gentle downhill power-glide, tires singing and spokes whistling as I raced along at the pace of a running deer. The day warmed quickly as I split each valley in search of the next. I shaped the *process* of bicycling into another piece in the assembly of the day. While I pedaled, I churned up the good feeling of powerful chemistry, all stirred up and bubbling hard. There are many miles to span, today. As I count them off, I feel satisfaction in marking off my progress.

And so it goes as I manufacture an entertaining day from the chore of getting from where I am to where I want to be. It's hard to escape a rut—hard to see each day as a new opportunity. Enjoying the ride is the secret to making each day count. *Intrepid* teaches me more of this magic all the time.

Moab buzzes with commerce. The natural surroundings are spectacular, but the city itself is somewhat sterile and functional. If you need to purchase gasoline, find lodging, get something to eat, repair your truck, pick up some recorded music, get film developed quickly, buy groceries or a new hat, browse for a magazine or book, wash your clothes, or get a cavity filled—Moab is your place. Its squared-off and lined-up face doesn't quite elevate the town to the level of "charming" or "interesting." But Moab is a fun-loving little city sitting in the middle of a magnificent region of exquisite geology.

Many "outfitters," backcountry tour guides for hire, base in Moab. I can understand why an outdoor enthusiast would search for a means to make Moab home. It must feel like heaven at times. The Colorado River slices off the northern edge of the city. Arches and Canyonlands National Parks stand to either side of Moab like supporting bookends. The lofty La Sal Mountains punctuate the morning-side skyline, and there are so many nifty nooks and corners tucked into the surrounding BLM lands it would be difficult to catalog them all. One could easily hike, bike and kayak into a constant state of euphoria while living in Moab. But I wonder if doing it commercially eventually dulls the experience.

After getting supplies, I continued north, crossing the Colorado River and climbing the five-mile grade to Arches National Park. The campground was another eighteen miles from the park entrance and 1,400 feet higher. The road to the campground began with a long low gear climb to a high plateau, followed by more moderate slopes punctuated with occasional glides. During the hot steep climb up the initial set of switchbacks that led away from the visitor center, a family in a van stopped beside me and handed me an icy soda.

I ran out of road with the sun still about thirty degrees high. Circling the campground, I picked an empty site next to an attractive woman who spoke with a German accent. She was with a guy who sounded regular American. After days of relative isolation, I thought this couple would be entertaining to observe. Later, they introduced themselves—Monika and Bruce. When you arrive on a bicycle, by yourself, people tend to follow their curiosity to your campsite. Monika and Bruce were just friends. Bruce lived in Salt Lake, and Monika was visiting from Germany. Bruce was very kind and invited me to join them for conversation.

Besides conversation, they also shared their dinner and their wine. I seldom drink any alcohol and even a small amount affects me. I tried to keep up with the details of their stories, but inevitably I found myself tuning out their words and just absorbing the music of Monika's voice while staring off at the stars hovering above the dimly outlined ridges.

Today I bicycled farther than ever before in a single day. A day that had begun as a slim notation between destinations had ended up being noteworthy. All things considered, it evolved into a splendid concoction nailed together from odds and ends scattered along the roadway.

Total mileage for the day: 88.3

## Days 13 and 14:

Two more friends, Cindy and Allen, joined Monika and Bruce. For two days, I hung out with this gang, hiking to several arches and to a steep gorge hidden deep in the backcountry, which plowed its way down to the Colorado River. Sitting atop one high ridge along the way, looking towards a hundred-mile horizon that was devoid of any visible sign of man's touch, Monika remarked that she could recall no spot in Europe that overlooked such a vast and rugged isolation as the one she now witnessed. She found it overpowering.

## Day 15—Mile 606:

I head south from Arches towards Canyonlands. My travel passes the point of becoming a long trip rather than just a trip. Austin seems far behind me, Santa Barbara distantly ahead of me. The good times I had in Arches and the short friendships I developed there have increased my feelings of loneliness and isolation although I am glad I had the chance to know these interesting people. I am reminded that in a strong sense, we are all transient. But my individual trek through life now seems especially fleeting. I am cramming each day, and, at times, days stretch uncannily—but each one is gone before I'm ready to release it. The last two weeks have lasted for six months. I am putting distance between my past and me. It's beginning to seem like I have always been pedaling down a highway. How can time be drawn and squeezed like this?

I especially miss Monika. She was mysterious and reminded me of a woman from my recent past. No—it is Barbara who I miss! How can that be? The many miles filled only by the one voice in my head have reeled a connection to the surface that I didn't realize was lurking below—or did not want to acknowledge. Should I tell Barbara my secret discovery?

I stopped for the night at the Cane Springs roadside park along US 191, south of Moab. This was a nice park, set well back from the highway, with water and restrooms and abundant large trees. And the area was scenic, with surrounding high cliffs.

Late that night, I awoke to loud crashes and yelling as three hooligans entered the isolated park and started busting up tables and such. Although the park was rather brightly lit, I lay out of view and tucked in the shadows. I had stretched my sleeping bag atop a fifteen foot high rock at the very back of the park. However, I had leaned *Intrepid* along the south side of a small shed near the back of the park, the side situated away from the expanse of the park, and the side on which the grass was much taller.

As I watched from my secret tower, the invaders began searching for limbs or boards or whatever they could scavenge to use as clubs, and one of them began searching towards the back of the park. I did not think I would be discovered directly, but I was very concerned my bike would be. Without it, I would be marooned in a very out of the way place, somewhere on planet Utah, where I knew not a single inhabitant to call upon. I grabbed my pump to use as a club and unfolded my large camping knife and prepared to defend my bicycle. I knew that if *Intrepid* were discovered, I might be, too—and I would be involved in a very serious struggle because I was witness to the vandalism that had now occupied these men for at least fifteen minutes.

The hooligan searching the back of the park for a club walked around to the rear of the shed after first trying to open the door. He was now only about four feet from *Intrepid* as he scanned the area below the rock where I perched. Outnumbered three to one, I was ready to attack with lethal force. Only one more corner of the shed concealed the location of my bike as I waited with thumping heart and shallow breath. Then, the drunken thug turned and wobbled back to the other two pathetic scoundrels. In another fifteen minutes, their rampage ended, and they staggered back to their pickup and drove away.

For the first time, I began to consider the vulnerability of being alone in a desolate and potentially hostile place—a vulnerability compounded by the fact that my vehicle was a flimsy twenty-three pound extension of myself.

Once the hoodlums left, I surveyed the park to discover only minimal damage. Probably very drunk, they inflicted more noise and fury than devastation. I moved my bike to a more remote hiding place and slipped into a shallower sleep.

# 7. Needles and Piñons

## Day 16:

The sweetness and stillness of the Utah morning is fractured here and there by the growl and stinky breath of speeding pickups as I pump southward along the narrow edge of U.S. Route191. The trucks and cars scurry past me in small convoys, the tails wanting to be the heads. The coming trains of vehicles cleave the silence several minutes before swooping past me, then fade in a long dying hiss.

Between the intermittent commotions, a hushed harmony backfills the ruts in the quiet carved by the vehicles. In the long calms between raids, a faint chorus resonates from my bike. The melody is not able to instantly penetrate the distances ahead of me like the snarl of a pickup but patiently travels along with me like a secret entrusted to a stealthy envoy passing through a hostile territory.

The inch-and-a-quarter bicycle tires hum reverently as they separate the asphalt into miles traveled from miles imagined. The chain lightly sings as it carries the energy of the engine within me from chain ring to cog. The spokes whistle in a whisper as they tussle the air that becomes my invisible wake.

At times, I can see ten miles of highway ahead of me and almost as much highway behind me. No one is there; nothing else is moving. I have the notion I could sit and meditate on the double yellow stripe that divides the road, but the scattered bits of road kill remind me of the folly in this notion. Reality comes in the form of deeply treaded Goodyears and chromed bumpers. I think of the irreverence of buzzards and ants. I calculate that all things material can be accounted for— but never reassembled once the spirit has fled.

The tranquility of morning soon evaporates in the boil and stir of the rising day. I ride on a fast grade towards Church Rock and the turnoff at Utah 211, the westward leg past Newspaper Rock and towards the end of the pavement at Canyonlands. I am impatient to make this junction, and I pedal hard against the building heat. Sweat is collecting under the band of my straw hat, and I tilt the hat back a little so the dampness can catch the breeze of my motion. I am not tired. I have become almost tireless, now. And the nervous energy generated in me by the indifferent buzz of passing vehicles pushes me along.

The bright yellow bag attached to the front of my handlebar has a clear-window map pocket on its top surface. Tucked into this pocket is a map, folded to show the options before me—and a compass that helps identify the twists and turns of my meandering route. Attached to a zipper on the bag is a small thermometer. Near the axle of the front wheel is an odometer that winds off both daily mileage and trip mileage. In their own ways, each of these things measures my progress.

Along the map is the bold red line labeled US 191. Given the events of the preceding night, the emblazoned line seems to indicate, "Danger!" I look ahead to the skinnier black and gray lines, on the map and in the distance. My body has become warrior hard, and I am losing the restraints of civilization. But I know that even warriors can be slain by unforgiving weapons and unthinking people. On this red highway, it would be easy enough to ride into oblivion in less than a wink. Life lived is always a gamble, but I would like to take my chances on the dead-end roads that few people travel.

I reach the junction with 211 at what I judge to be mid morning, and I make the turn westward. In this country, going in a westerly direction almost always means pedaling into the wind, and this time is no exception.

The westward trek begins with a long steady climb to a summit that would probably have a name in a less spectacular land. On a bike, this is the type of summit that you can see a long time before you get there. In the face of a hot headwind, it is a tough climb. The climb is not so much of a physical challenge as it is a mental one. My progress towards the summit seems slow, so I look back and measure my escape from 191, instead.

I am looking for patience. My mind wanders. I am struck by the irony of traveling so far, with so much effort and risk, only to have my mind retreat to another place and time. And so my thoughts dance from here to there—from now to then—weaving an intricate pattern that will forever change what I am. How will another ever know what I have become without doing this too?

As I look ahead to the summit, I can see a lone house built along the ridgeline to the north of the highway, perhaps a quarter mile from the road. As I approach, I determine the structure is abandoned. The house is simple but very nice, with a grand covered porch. I can see through the large windows, all the way through the house, front-to-rear. The windows face the expansive horizons towards sunrise and sunset provided by the house's ridge-top location. Was it too lonely in this place even with the company of family and two dogs in the yard?

At the apex of the grade, I look back to the distant black line of red 191, scribed across the hard scrabble of Utah, then go over to the backside of the ridge towards the end of the little black line on my map.

With gravity to my back and shelter from the wind provided by the more convoluted terrain, my pace is much faster now. Away from the ridge, the surrounding hillsides grow ever taller and nearer, collecting themselves into the walls of a broad canyon that swallows me. I wind down a set of steep switchbacks and then follow a shaded stream. There is only one way back out. So I know that I must later traverse this long glide in reverse, as a climb. But onward I sail, past the picnic tables (too early for lunch) beneath the stands of cottonwoods at Newspaper Rock, tattooed with ancient petroglyphs and more recent graffiti. Finally, I settle to the bottom of the grade and into a long march that off-and-on exchanges a succession of little ups for little downs. I am looking for a rhythm to carry me and trying to be within myself.

The road is empty. Not a single vehicle has passed me since I left 191 more than an hour behind me. A few dirt roads trickle off to one side of the highway or the other, hinting at hidden outposts. Mostly there are no fences along the highway, but sometimes a fence-line crosses the road, punctuating it with the throb of a cattle guard. The highway follows the bottom of a broad meandering canyon whose walls grow taller as I progress. In places, the canyon walls fall away where prominent side-canyons intersect it. I enjoy the scenery but look ahead to the park—still trying to be within myself. It's been a long ride, it seems, although I am not physically challenged by it. Why am I so impatient?

A face lingers in my mind, the young woman left behind but discovered along the highway. Her eyes had pierced me deeply with secret primordial forces—a relationship implied but never spoken, never pursued, barely imagined. Barbara exuded a quality that exposed a simple harmonic resonance, a fundamental that could not be further explained. She created a secret seed: deliberately, subtly, and indelibly. I doubt she realized her power. Acknowledging it would have been inappropriate, and I never did. Yet, out here where all the consequences can be

safely abandoned, I understand that the resonance was very true—
even though denied. Perhaps it is the mystery of her that lingers in me.
I was not thinking of her when I left Austin. Her image has found me
here, in this isolation.

I am into the afternoon, and I am looking for a place to stop for
lunch. I finally spot a solitary tree with good shade about a hundred
yards off the north side of the road. Why is it here? I carry Intrepid
across the sand, weaving a bit through the scattered shrubs. I prop my
bike against the trunk of the tree and free one pannier from the rack on
the back of my bike. From the handlebar bag, I take a letter that I had
started writing, along with my knife and a canteen filled with tea. Then I
sit in the shade of the tree, upon a surprisingly cool rock, half buried in
the sand. Fishing in the pannier, I net a can of meat, a sourdough roll,
and zip-lock bag of slightly melted cheese. Then I build a very plump
sandwich that threatens to spill out around the slice in the roll.

As I slowly eat my sandwich, I am struck by each individual taste:
the sourness of the bread, the saltiness of the meat and the
tanginess of the cheese. My tea, although kept in an insulated bottle,
is no cooler than was the morning air. The wetness of each swallow
seems to defy the desert that engulfs me. Around me, the view is
sifted into layers: mountains rising to the south above rumpled walls of
closer cliffs; distant mesas ahead partially eclipsed by intervening
hogbacks; the nearby bottom strewn with contorted boulders awash in
a rolling river of sandbars. I am speared by a sense of depth—of the
various distances being lined up in a sequence—of being immersed in
the near and the far.

Something about the improvised nature of my little roadside "park"
weaves me into the landscape—places me here; renders me absent from
wherever else I might have been. I am a participant and not an observer.
All of my senses seem to hang in suspended animation as if giving me
the chance to linger in each sensation—flowing, yet standing still.

I review the letter, and I picture the intuitive, shy young woman who
rose from a mirage to ambush me on the lonely highway. She's out
there now, in another place. The image in my head takes on sudden
depth and life. I speak to her in a voice barely above a whisper: "Barbara,
in the unlikely event that we ever meet again, I will be eye-to-eye and
direct with you. Ambiguity will be erased. The seed you created will no
longer be a secret, and your power will be revealed."

I realize this journey is changing me. Within me, the simplest and most instinctive truths of human reality now challenge the polite and reasoned conventions of society. People will likely find me irrational, and I may be left with thirst that can never be quenched. The aftermath of this trip could leave me more isolated than the remoteness of this land.

I finish writing the letter to Barbara and give fair warning of the changes in me. I realize this letter is like shouting at the ocean or the moon. Although the letter itself will not produce a tangible outcome in terms of shaping events, the writing of it has a measurable effect on my perspective.

The impatience in me has ebbed, for now. I understand that the answers I seek are farther away than I can possibly ride.

After awhile, I repack the stuff onto *Intrepid* and head back for the road. As I hoist my loaded bike to my shoulder, I feel the power and spring of my legs. I know that I am a small and fragile entity in a large and uncaring universe, and all that I am will be lost in the eons that follow— but on this day, I have the strength and will to carry myself all the way to the end of the highway. It may not matter, but I will do it anyway.

When I crest the final hill before reaching the park, there is no doubt that I have arrived. The view ahead is expansive and spectacular. The cliffs are taller and more imposing. Some are almost blood red. I ride past the marker at the park entrance and on to the trailer that serves as the park headquarters. I pay for a campsite and then pedal to the low, knuckled butte at Squaw Flat and the semi-primitive campground that skirts it.

Squaw Flat Campground extends a safe harbor after the long tacks south and west—but not too safe. I am, after all, at the bitter end of a long road that goes nowhere else, with limited supplies. I must hurdle a challenging ride back to 191, followed by a stiff climb into lofty Monticello.

But these tests that lie ahead worry me less than the longing that squirms into my sleeping bag with me as the deep black of a Canyonlands night descends upon my little tent. Out the screen, above my head, I can see Cygnus flying along the Milky Way—and my flight feels just as long.

Total mileage for the day: 67.4

## Day 17:

Things must interact one with another in order to exist. Without interaction, everything would dissolve into nothing. One way to create a vacuum is to cease all interaction. According to one interpretation of Quantum Mechanics, a thing does not exist unless it is observed. Until the moment of observation, there is only a probability that the thing *might exist*.

The campground at Squaw Flat is large and spread out around two loose loops. There are not a lot of campsites, and in most, one cannot see the neighboring campsites. I camped along the eastern loop, facing the morning sun. The campsites strung along this loop are all backed into individual alcoves as the dead end road winds north to south following the meandering eastern face of the butte. This section of the campground is not really a "loop." It only has a tiny loop at the end of it. And there are no facing campsites on the other side of the road. Thus, the view to the rising sun is an uninter-rupted bounce across Squaw Flat, a wide meadow covered in tall grass and subtle wild flowers that sparkle in the early morning sun with an almost imagined hint of dew.

Beyond the meadow are low silhouettes of broad, carved mesas, their banded colors disguised in shadows and the piercing glare of the sun. In the clear air, the sun is welding torch bright even as it hangs low in the sky. A few miles away, the barrel-like spires of North and South Six Shooter Peaks take wild aim at the morning.

The campground is nearly empty in early September. The days are still hot, and the fleeting mornings are to be cherished. The night had been eerily quiet and still. I heard the night patrol of a few small critters, and then I was swallowed by a deep but slightly troubled sleep. I cannot recall the nature of the conflict. I only feel the aftermath, a slight disquiet. My dreams are far within me, too far for me to see them. But the feelings leak out in the dawn.

Today, I will hike. I have prepared for a quick getaway. Last night, I chained *Intrepid* to the picnic table in my campsite and filled my canteens at the water truck. I walked for water in the darkness and almost stepped on a small rattlesnake in the process. It buzzed me sternly, and I froze in mid-stride, switching on my flashlight in time to see it slide backwards and turn. I knew to use my flashlight for walking in the evening, but I was enjoying the darkness and the starlit canopy above. Instinctively, I was alert for movement and sound, and reacted quickly. I made a note in my head to not be complacent.

Being *here and now* is a big part of my quest. The stars connect me to many bits of washed-up wreckage, and tides of memory and dream sweep me away whenever I look at a starry night sky. The little pygmy rattler chided me for drifting off to another place and time.

Awareness is the wine squeezed from the grapes of reality. It is partly about being in the moment and place that you are. But when and where are you? Seeing with the mind's eye is also essential—seeing over the horizon to reckon your place, and seeing the beginning and end to sequence the moment. Sensing and interpreting: welding these disparate parts into a single vision is the essence of awareness. The sensing part of this double vision gives me trouble—keeping the mind from wandering off from the body.

Today needs more attention. Today I am in Canyonlands, and here at the end of the road where great rivers collide in the void on the map, beyond the reach of the last telephone line, it is clear I must settle into the day I have at hand. With only my bicycle to carry me, there is simply no easy escape. I will have to accept it.

I quickly packed food and canteens and found a trail heading south from the campground. Much of Canyonlands is broken into shuffled pieces, some piled a little higher than others. The trails sometime wind opportunistically over low ridges that separate sandy soil flats. The flats seem to me like gardens in gigantic pots, ringed by sandstone walls and self-contained.

Here and there along the ridges, I encountered potholes within the rock that had become filled with soil. In some, plants have taken root to create miniatures of the sandy meadows that stretch between the many intersecting ridges. Part of my fitting into the day became the search for parallels between the large and the small, looking for the tenacious footholds where life expands unexpectedly. I was searching for things that could only be seen from where I was standing or sitting and letting my thoughts slow to a pace where I could examine each one of them.

Canyonlands has a lumpy, broken face. Deep beneath the surface, massive deposits of salt and gypsum have been compromised, causing the overlying layers of rock to sag and fracture. The gnawing, eating, and prying of flowing, standing, and freezing water—together with the whittling of blowing sand—have widened the fractures and sculpted the rocks into a labyrinth of shadowy canyons, secret basins, enclosing fortresses, dissected chambers, and haunting faces and figures frozen in the rock. Some of the ridgelines are broken and eroded into needle-like spires that give this section of the park its name.

Each time I cross a ridge, I stop to note the view all around. The Needles District does not have an obvious overlook point. I normally target the highest vista point in a park, but here I am forced to evaluate the nuances of each little summit as I cross it. Many only reveal the topography of the neighborhood. Some have more distant views in various directions but are obscured in other directions. Every once in a while a high point surprises me with a vista having a nearly circular reach into the distance. Even at the best of these points, most of the horizon is truncated by higher terrain within twenty or thirty miles of my vantage. To the north float Junction Butte and the Island in the Sky. Chopping the horizon to the east are the alpine-like La Sal Mountains, the higher mesas of Arches, and the general incline towards Colorado. To the south rise the forested slopes of the nearby Abajo Mountains. And off maybe forty miles to the west are the colorful Henry Mountains.

It's a big view, but one that is still somewhat containing. I bicycled around the Henry Mountains enroute from Capital Reef to Lake Powell. I try to recall the view from there to here, connecting it with what I see from here to there.

The subtle fragrances of morning evaporate quickly into the day. The localized chill of sweat replaces the coolness of surrounding air. I march fast but take time to stop where the view is good or details catch my attention.

My objective for the day is to hike a long loop, south from the campground to Chesler Park, west through the narrow passages of The Joints, then back north and a little east, returning by way of Elephant Hill. As I turn back towards Elephant Hill from the far end of my hike, the sun blankets the landscape with the ooze of a slow bake. Sunlight reflecting from the sandstone begins to toast me, even beneath the brim of my straw cowboy hat. It was time to do what any smart lizard would do: find some shade.

I locate deep shade on the north face of a substantial cliff, a spot that can only be reached obliquely by the rays of the early morning sun. The rocks are cool, and I have a lofty view from northwest through north, and on to the east. I will hibernate in this coolness for most of the afternoon. Taking my cue from the previous day, I build my sandwich in anticipation of a sensuous and savored event.

I perch with enough elevation to see across the voids carved by the Green and Colorado Rivers, and beyond to the steeply chiseled crowns of Ekker and Elaterite Buttes, and the Buttes of the Cross (named by John Wesley Powell who explored the rivers in 1869 and 1871). Candlestick Tower anchors off the shore of the Island in the Sky. I am not in a hurry. I lay my head on my pack and take a nap. Instead of dreaming of another place, I wish Barbara to be here.

*Junction Butte and the Island in the Sky*

I arrived back in camp in time to bike to an overlook at the end of the scenic drive to catch the sunset. The drive extends about three miles north from the campground. The view from the Big Spring Overlook, at the end of the road, is quite restricted, but there are impressive vistas available from the nearby highpoints. However, finding a highpoint that is climbable is a bit of a trick. I found a good one to the northwest of the parking area: up the dry wash a short ways, on the left side of the wash. From the top of the little tower, I stole a good all-around view, including the magnificent buttes bearing west through the north.

When I got back to my campsite, the couple camped next to me came over and introduced themselves and offered me cold orange juice. These nice folks from the western slope of Colorado had noticed my comings and goings on my bicycle but had seen no car or truck at my campsite. They were curious.

I visited with the Colorado couple until it was quite dark, then left the narrow, night-blinded perimeter blazed by their Coleman lantern for the dimmer and subtler borders of my own campsite. Once my eyes adjusted, I could see faint silhouettes around the horizon shouldering bales of stars. I didn't linger in the darkness, falling asleep as soon as I stretched out on my sleeping bag.

## Day 18:

I awoke early this morning with a feeling of anticipation. I biked to the end of the scenic drive where I chained my *Intrepid* to a post. From there, I hiked the twenty-mile roundtrip to Confluence Overlook, high above the point where the Green and Colorado rivers entangle to flow onward into Cataract Canyon, united as a mightier Colorado.

Confluence Overlook is one of those places that anchor the map— a place that you can point to on a photo of Earth taken from space orbit and say, "I was there."

The sweeping majesty of this point is worthy of its pivotal position. Snaking its way in from the northeast, the Colorado River drains most of the western slope of the state of Colorado, as well as much of northeastern Utah. Meandering down from the northwest, the Green River empties much of northern Utah. Where they collide, each river is locked to its course by the vertical walls of twisting, quarter-mile deep canyons. Empowered by the combined force of the two great rivers, the enlarged Colorado plunges a straighter course through the high, sandstone plateau as it grinds the depths of Cataract Canyon, downstream from the confluence.

From Confluence Overlook, one can clearly see the division of a vast land. The Y-shaped slicing of the highlands is displayed in staggering detail. The eye can follow the tops of the winding canyons as they cross the wide plateau. The blind rivers below were first guided to a common meeting point by the hand of gravity about thirteen million years ago. On the north side, between the branches of the "Y", rise the towering red cliffs and buttes of the Island in the Sky. To the west sprawls the immense labyrinth of the Maze. On the east side, I sit upon the broken-off shore of the Needles.

Through eons, cycles of water poured over the land, chopping and dicing the whole of this harsh landscape. Occasional torrents extract a toll when added over great time. Runoff, directed by gravity into the open veins and arteries splayed across the faces of the rock formations, gathers into ever-larger channels, becoming a flood. Momentum building and stained red, brown, and yellow with innumerable shards of sand, the currents become deeper and steeper, faster and more turbulent—ripping and tearing at the beds and banks of the channels. Gravity heaps the scattered confusion across the great basins into concentrated assaults. The tireless flows at the bottoms of the great gorges convey the debris downstream, grinding and sawing as they haul the load—deepening the well of gravity. Even now, I can hear the groaning and splashing of the river far below me as it toils under gravity's whip.

I see the first cumulus of afternoon forming over the escarpments of the Island in the Sky. Caught in a rift of time, I see the darkening of thousands of afternoon skies—hear the booming thunder echoing from the cliffs—see the spears of lightning stabbing the ground with heat like the Sun's—see clouds torn open and spilling—hear the floods boring through the canyons. Over and over across the millennia, gravity conspired with the lifting energy of the sun to split the enumerable tiny bonds that build the vastness of far-flung places. All the scattered points of the immense Colorado/Green River Basin are connected to the canyon imprisoned confluence below me by the web of streams and inevitable rivers that sculpt the land and concentrate the life-giving waters. From this magical vantage point far from the highway, tucked within a blank area on the roadmap, I am gripped by the workings of planet Earth—longer than I can remember, longer than I will ever know.

The confluence summoned me. Before my journey began, a large topographic map of the Canyonlands hung above my bed. I remember sleepless nights when the light of the Moon beamed through the open curtains to illuminate the contours of the canyons and the tracts of the rivers. I recall the strong feeling that life was out there somewhere, passing me by. I still feel the chill and the tears of those hours. I had to go search for the deserted waypoint where I now sit. The answers are not here—but the connections might be.

By laying the progress of one day against the progress of another, I came to this point of dreams by bicycle and foot. I depart towards a destination less defined—but somehow chiseled by the call and the trek to the confluence of the Green and Colorado.

*The point that called me in the moonlight in Austin*

When I returned to camp, I discovered an animal had chewed into one of the panniers I hid in some bushes before leaving. It chewed right through the nylon zipper, as well as the pack cloth near the top of the main pocket. The Colorado couple occupying the next campsite gave me moral support, safety pins for repairs, and a tasty, hot supper.

**Day 19:**

I decided not to bicycle on the Indian reservations in the Four Corners area because of many warnings against doing so by people I met. While not convinced I would have a problem, the events at Cane Springs pushed me in the direction of caution. Instead, I would detour into Colorado then drop down to Chaco Canyon in New Mexico.

Whatever loosely conceived plan I started with at the beginning of my trip was now completely discarded. From day to day, I had little idea of what my destination would be or by what route I would get there. Points to the west of me almost seemed like they were on the other side of a can't-get-there-from-here breach in the map. The detour north into Arches was a spontaneous addition in response to the fact that I was covering more distance each day than anticipated. It was a bonus of sorts. But this unexpected detour to the east, away from my ultimate goal of reaching Santa Barbara, was something completely different—more like hitting a wall that I didn't know was there and bouncing off in a direction I never considered.

I biked to Monticello and got a room for the night at a small motel. From Monticello, I made calls to Eileen, a friend in Austin with whom I had frequently taken hiking trips. She was interested in meeting me at Chaco Canyon and also wanted to drive to Mesa Verde. Her plan, as she developed it that evening, was to fly into Albuquerque and get a rental car. But it would be a week before she could meet me.

The thought of a good friend sharing some of my adventure and plying me with something more than "Hello, how are you?" conversation for a few days buoyed my spirit.

I still did not know how I was going to get from one side of the map to the other without riding across the Indian lands, but for the moment I could focus elsewhere.

Total mileage for the day: 53.2

**Day 20:**

I biked to Cortez, getting rained upon four or five times in the process. As I peddled from Utah to Colorado, I watched the granite peaks of the La Platas rise above the arc of the Earth, their serrated ridges replacing the high plateaus along the northern and eastern horizons. Ahead loomed Mesa Verde, the imposing tabletop mountain that once sheltered a lost world of the Anasazi.

I stayed in a motel in Cortez and called Eileen to make final arrangements for our rendezvous at Chaco Canyon.

Total mileage for the day: 66.3

## Day 21:

Eileen would meet me in Chaco Canyon on Day 27, so I had a few days to fill and no plan how I would do that. The day at hand took on a slow, less-than-purposeful pace.

Near the town of Mancos, I encountered two teenage cyclists headed in the opposite direction. They were ready for a short break, so the three of us detoured to a store nearby.

These two guys had just graduated from high school a few months earlier and were on a coast-to-coast trip from their homes in Connecticut to San Diego. They had already traveled 2,600 miles, mostly over flat terrain, and were still adjusting to the mountainous region they had now entered.

They were "motel camping," and they somewhat marveled at the heavy load I was carrying. The motel-to-motel strategy lightened and streamlined their loads. It also allowed them to make quick starts in the mornings. Moreover, they could continue riding late in the day because they could reserve accommodations that were closely spaced in virtually every town along their chosen route. The daily certainty of a safe stopping point, located at a well-spaced interval in the overall scheme of their ride, was a huge difference between their trip and mine. Actually, I wasn't sure that my trip still had a scheme. Okay, I still had a destination: Santa Barbara. I just wasn't pedaling in that direction (as the two youthful riders helpfully pointed out to assist with my navigation).

By contrast, the two young cyclists were pointed toward their destination of San Diego. They would have to cross the Navajo Reservation, much as I originally intended. I listened as they explained that they were not worried. Yeah, but who worries when you're eighteen? Besides, there were two of them. And they were traveling light and fast.

And if they did not show up at the motel in the evening, someone would start looking for them.

We had ice cream and left in opposite directions. I was still chewing on the contradictions and gaps in my "plan."

As I climbed rather lazily into the elevations of Colorado, I could see the vegetation zone fade from the piñons and junipers, which had become so familiar in Utah, into Ponderosa pines and Aspens, a transition that was evident not only to the eye but also to the nose. I daydreamed about venturing into the high mountains to the north—a dangerous thought maybe. It didn't seem like a serious consideration, merely an entertaining meander of the mind.

I stopped for the night at a national forest campground that was too close to the highway to be truly pleasant. And I stopped much too early in the day to be satisfied with my progress. I had the feeling I was just hanging out, and I hated it.

Total mileage for the day: 25.8 Total mileage for the trip: 821

## Day 22:

I woke up in a fussy mood. I needed a plan. I could not loiter any longer.

The morning started with a dousing from a brief thunderstorm that rolled over the ridgeline. Leftover clouds lingered overhead, and I was circling in a bit of a cloud inside me. For the moment, I would just start riding. Turning the pedals would be the first step in any plan, so I would just start riding. A plan would come to me if I just kept turning the crank. I aimed towards Durango, but my mind drifted.

Perspective. The same action is not the same experience to all people. One person looks into a mountain valley, taken by the sweep, and sees a colorful landscape. Another looks into the same valley and witnesses a collage of interrelated parts. One person measures the angles, contours and elevations while another measures his or her place in the scheme of things. One person will see a plan; another person will see mystery. Some measure the universe against themselves. Others measure themselves against the universe. It is hard for me to imagine that any person would not be changed by a trip like mine, but I do not think that the nature of the change can be predicted. Personal perspective.

The reality around us cannot be judged in a single way, and the basic elements seem to change after weeks of churning away on the seat of a bicycle. The complications of modern living fragment one's consciousness into individual tasks that become purposes unto themselves. A person grasps one-handed onto a run-away train, pulled along at a pace that is too fast to hop aboard, too fast to let go. A central meaning or awareness can escape a person, and then, channeled by expectations, she or he gets pressed into place and stitched to an outline scratched in a photograph that is supposed to theirs. Perspective lost.

The way others see a person creates its own reality. Disconnecting opens possibilities for new connections. Traveling on skinny, spoked wheels and personal resolve crunches old realities and spawns new ones. Is it detail or perspective that I am gaining? Can I fit back into the space in the photos that others have left for me? Would I even consider it? Details noted. Perspective found.

I reached the high summit at Hesperus. Patches of sunlight quilted the valley and ranges beyond. The last long stretch of downhill highway into town lighted my senses. I sailed into Durango humming *Ode to Joy*.

I decided to tackle the mighty San Juan Mountains, but first I would ride to Chaco Canyon and hike for a few days while waiting for Eileen to arrive.

*A puddle grants a fleeting opportunity for a toehold*
*on life in the desert*

# 8. Messengers

## More Day 22:

Durango sparkles with interesting and fun things and would be a great place to live if it didn't snow so darn much! The people who live here project that it is their favorite spot on Earth. The atmosphere is relaxed but thoughtful. Sprinkled among the residents are city people who have decided to live without the city. Dress leans towards casual, and movement is unhurried and deliberate. Lunch assumes a ritual: time to walk around town, visit engaging shops, or have a glass of wine with friends. Cars are for tourists, except on weekends when the four-by-four takes you into the mountains.

Durango is vibrant and in demand. The shops are a statement by the proprietors about their satisfaction with earning a living in this outpost on the fringes of the modern world. No quarter of town yields any sense of moving up or moving on. This is home as it was in a daydream back in the city where the office walls loomed as gray as rain. And Durango exudes history, exciting history that even lends a stranger passing through town a sense of borrowed roots. The old steam trains and the old buildings provide visible reminders of the spirited mining days that are not too hard to imagine, especially given the still wild terrain surrounding the town.

The approach of an intense thunderstorm drove me out of Durango. My next destination was Farmington, New Mexico.

Farmington was like purgatory after Durango, all function and no imagination. The drivers rudely swooped close to my bike even when no other vehicles were within sight. What was the source of this hostility?

The stores in Farmington were mostly of the chain variety, and the buildings wore rectangular faces without expression. I was, however, thankful to find a Schwinn bike shop. Schwinn shops have been the only bike shops I've encountered, and not every town has one. Both tires on my bike were new at the start of my trip, but the rear one was completely worn out by the time I got to Farmington. The man at the Schwinn shop surprised me when he did not ask about my travel despite the long-distance touring gear fastened to my bike.

I guess that summed up Farmington: a town without curiosity. The sky was ready to open up with rain again, so I decided to avail myself to more of the bare functionality the town provided. I got a motel room and spent the night in Farmington, anyway.

## Day 23:

If you count turns of the crank, you will quickly grow weary from the ride—any ride that you take. Passion drains into habit, tediously clung to, tediously measured. Relationships, marriage, career, a favorite restaurant—the spark is doused by the hypnosis of counting strokes. Making more strokes becomes the purpose. We miss the prizes of life by simply looking down too much, losing sight of the mysteries along the wayside.

Perspective.

The morning struggled out of the darkness in the pall of the continuing rain. I was getting tired of the rain and wanted to get to Chaco today, but this was hopeless. It was hard *not* to look down in the rain.

I waited out one shower at a small museum at Salmon Ruins, just outside Bloomfield. The local residents and the county provided most of the support for this subtle, unpretentious museum revolving around the remains of an outlying village of the Chaco people.

At the museum I met a couple from Fort Collins, Colorado, that was touring on a tandem bicycle. Tandems are highly efficient touring machines. Moreover, the company of another person provides a propellant more powerful than the extra set of legs. It was the couple's first such trip, and *their* bike and all *their* gear looked new and pristine. They left the museum in a light rain, covered by matching ponchos and chattering happily.

I carried dreams and a longing. At times these fueled me, but I was still alone.

I waited for the rain to quit. The contrast struck by the couple on the tandem bike shook my spirit—the contrast of solitary versus female/male shared. The grayness of the day was deepened by this contrast. Part of me seemed to be suddenly missing, lagging behind somewhere along the long road.

The event signaled more than a mere shift in my mood. It exposed two very different realities to life. I would not be able to simply dismiss the feeling. I understood I was knocking the dust off realities that had been tucked into the corners or pushed to the back shelves of my life. My trip was about rearranging and disposing of various realities. But first, I had to knock off the dust.

The rain stopped, but the sky did not clear. I left the museum and headed south from Bloomfield. After a while, it started to rain again, and a headwind rose. Then my bubble burst. I had a flat, or at least my bike did. I stood beside the road listening to the indifferent roar of passing pickups, staring almost catatonically at the limp rear tire. Rear tire—damn! It was almost *always* the rear tire, so much harder to fix than the front one. I cursed the rain. I cursed the wind. I cursed the flat tire. I just stood there.

Where was that second supportive voice? "Honey, it's only a flat tire. It won't rain forever. The wind will be to our backs tomorrow."

After several minutes in this graveyard of discouragement, I managed, almost by habit, to fix the flat tire. Without anything else to do, I mounted my bike and began to pedal. In the absence of inspiration, the sheer momentum of repetition set me into motion.

Perspective had ridden by on tandem bike. Life is what you make it. It is built one situation at a time. No single event can make your life what you want it to be. Sometimes the ride is a search. To find joy, one must recognize the treasures encountered along the road. The search is meaningless without the recognition.

As darkness swamped the gray skies, I found a spot beside the highway where my tent would be inconspicuous. Inside my cocoon, I intended to ignore the world unless it came in after me. I fell asleep amongst the wails of coyotes and the roar of speeding semis.

## Day 24:

The morning did not break with clear skies as I had hoped. At least it wasn't raining, and the clouds were thinning. The wind still abraded forward motion, but I *could* ride. Riding would change my situation.

I worked steadily, almost mechanically, against the incline and the elements, and I tried to remain oblivious to the all-too-close traffic. The incline and the elements didn't bother me as much as being buzzed by traffic. I was annoyed to still be on a road connecting two places with people going from one place to the other in a hurry. I preferred roads that few people considered and that went nowhere fast.

Before my stupor could degenerate into pessimism, I reached the junction with New Mexico 57, the dirt road leading to Chaco, twenty-nine miles away. Although not paved, the road proved good enough for slow riding and traffic was almost nonexistent. While I rode, the sky broke apart in splashes of blue and the rolling terrain became a rumpled patchwork of light and shadow. I reminded myself I was on vacation—a partial truth. I was entering the outback again. As quickly as the isolation grew, as quickly as the sunshine drenched me, the ride felt fun again. A different road can lead to a big change in perspective.

Just before reaching the park, I approached a bridge spanning a dry wash. The bridge was in poor condition, so I dismounted to walk across it. As I got off my bike, I noticed two graves beside the road. Each had been covered with a separate pile of stones, mounded up from the earth—shallow graves in a brick-hard land. These were not civilized graves blessed by a church. These were graves of necessity. These were graves of stark reality. The heaped-up graves of rock outlined the lives lost within. Both graves were marked by 2 x 4 crosses: one roughly nailed together and the other smoothed, carefully jointed and varnished. The first cross lacked inscription of any kind; the second was carefully carved.

Tired and without conscious thought, I stared at the second marker. Suddenly, the realization struck me that the cross measured out thirty-one years to its bearer.

Thirty-one years—my age. I rubbed my face wearily and stared a moment more.

"Jesse R. Valdez, who the hell are you, and what are you doing buried here in this lonely place with a nameless companion?"

I wanted to know but then again, I didn't want to know.

"There'll be no dying today, Jesse." And I left.

In this desolate place, I understood like I had never understood before. Life is short—and it is played for keeps.

# 9. Chaco

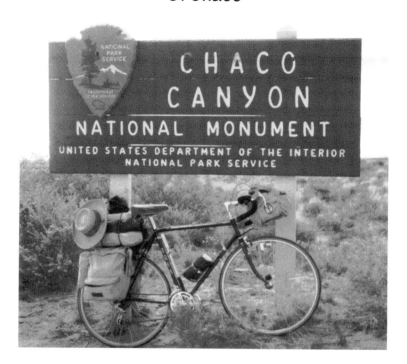

Twenty thousand years ago, human eyes scanned the Milky Way from the broad floor of Chaco Canyon. Even today, the clear, moonless night skies above Chaco are dark and filled with the speckled specters of thousands of stars. To the eye, the bowl of night has not changed over the millennia.

And even today, Chaco remains a hidden and isolated place. The long bike ride into the canyon along the desolate dirt road emphasizes the remoteness of this lost outpost. Our modern world bypassed this shallow canyon and the surrounding plateau, but nomadic bands of ancient hunters found this place again and again. Chaco provided relative sanctuary in the vastness of the continent that was untamed and mostly unpopulated.

The landscape of Chaco was wetter and greener in those days. Large game was abundant, providing kills to feed the tribes of Paleo Indians that passed through the region in search of great herds of animals. Over thousands of years, the climate changed and the land began to dry towards desert. The roaming tribes became smaller, hunting and gathering to provide the sustenance of life. Nomadic life is harsh even in familiar territory. And when these people acquired an advanced technology that allowed them to settle in one place, Chaco was a place that many chose as home.

This advanced technology was agriculture, a technology based upon a number of innovations. The implications were enormous.

To appreciate how a culture can be carved out of nothing but the human spirit and the raw wilderness, we cannot roll back the hands of time from our current place in history. We must look forward from the beginning and try to imagine the blackness of those nights long ago and the emptiness, not only of the continent, but also of the vault of human invention. Perspective.

Among the wandering tribes of hunter-gatherers, important technologies included stone spear points, throwing sticks that added leverage to the hurling of spears, clothing made from animal skins, piercing and cutting implements fashioned from bone, and fire. And the ancient ones must also have had a language that allowed them to work cooperatively.

Shelters were temporary and crude, sometimes just a natural alcove within the face of a cliff. If constructed, a shelter was probably a simple pit house made by applying mud to a stacked wooden framework erected over a shallow excavation with a fire pit dug near the center, and a hole in the roof to provide access for the occupants and escape for the smoke from the fire.

Even for larger groups consisting of a hundred or more of these ancient nomads, the feelings of vulnerability and isolation must have been extremely powerful. Forces far beyond their understanding shaped each day of their lives. Death was a constant traveling partner; its inevitability was weaved into virtually every pursuit and every ritual. Exploration was done one footstep at a time. Home was where the herds of big game were. The herds moved; they moved.

Day was divided from the night by the sun. There was no deeper reason. Winter followed the summer because the sun retreated to the south. Proper homage would bid its return. The fires of stars twinkle from the dome of night which was mysteriously, like sunsets and rainbows, always beyond walking distance. Storms were the fury and the gifts of gods; no other explanation could suffice.

Folklore, mythology, and even religion became yet other technologies that aided survival, added comfort, and provided meaning to the harsh reality of this primitive lifestyle.

Thus, these ancestral nomads living in obscurity on the declining fringes of the last ice age, constantly in pursuit of big game, were not without important inventions that separated them, across a wide gulf of sophistication, from the other creatures of Earth. The inventions surely did not come quickly or easily, nor did the social groupings that allowed these inventions to be concentrated and applied.

I grope to understand these beginnings. When trying to imagine them, I wind the clock backward from where I am now. But looking backward in this way simply does not reveal the ingenuity and persistence of these ancient people. It is so hard to see the darkness of those nights: hard to imagine a world without roads or maps; hard to imagine the solitude in the whine of the ancient winds; very hard to imagine the emptiness of the human toolbox; hard to know what it felt like to see the smoke of an unknown campfire rising against a distant horizon; hard to imagine the awkwardness when one tribe encountered another. Perspective. Same place—different time.

By comparison, my twenty-three pound bicycle is a marvel of high technology. It is to the technology of those ancient people what a jet aircraft is to my bicycle. The materials and the mechanisms would simply be beyond ancient comprehension. The efficiency of its wheels, bearings and multiple gears would simply be magical.

My clothing, my tent of synthetic fabrics, my zippered down sleeping bag, my compass, maps, and my stainless steel knife all connect me to people and industry over the horizon. Roads connect me with certainty from one point to another. In a small pannier, I carry food for a week with energy, nutrition and purity unavailable to the ancients. On my bicycle and with my lightweight equipment, I sail the backcountry roads with swift abandon, covering more distance in a day than the ancient tribes could have covered in two weeks. I am well fueled, jet-swift, and potently aware. And I sleep warm, dry, and protected from insects. I cannot be alone in the way that these early people were alone.

More than anything else—more than roads and manufactured equipment, more than packaged food and watered campgrounds, and more than a common language to greet encountered strangers—what prevents me from seeing Chaco from the perspective of a prehistoric nomad is the knowledge within my head. No matter how hard I try, I cannot blank out what I already know. The greatest divide is the one least tangible.

Mystery surrounds me, but I must look harder to find it than did the ancient ones. Traveling alone on a bicycle, my solitude and vulnerability are quite real, but I remain connected. Pondering these prehistoric visitors to Chaco has added a new perspective to my wanderings, but I realize that it is not their perspective—not even close.

The traces of the earliest occasional occupants of Chaco are subtle and hidden. However, there is nothing subtle about the ruins left behind by their Anasazi descendants, dating backward from one to two thousand years. Many of the tapered stone walls of their apartment-like pueblos still stand against the elements in silent tribute to the industry and skill of the Anasazi who built them. In some cases, the dwellings, work areas and ceremonial halls of an entire community, ranging into the thousands of inhabitants, are consolidated neatly into a single pueblo structure.

What filled the gap between the nomadic big game hunters and the great "cities" of the Anasazi? A succession of many new technologies allowed the tribes to stay in one location and concentrate upon further refinements to their way of life. They became connected to Chaco and learned to exploit its resources.

Leading the way into this bold, new reality was the acquisition of simple agriculture, at first just a supplement to the hunting and gathering. The crops consisted of corn and squash and were probably very unreliable in the beginning. The new, settled lifestyle was advanced by the inventions of baskets and pottery that were useful in storing food and water. Irrigation increased the yields of crops and improved reliability. Trade was developed with tribes over the horizon, especially to the south. Beans were acquired, and the diet of the Chacoans was dramatically enriched. The bow and arrow were also introduced, and the hunting of small game became a profitable enterprise. Meat now supplemented agriculture.

Shelter designs were revised. First, the pit houses were enlarged and improved, sometimes incorporating multiple rooms and better entryways. Then the ancient ones developed the great stone and adobe pueblos and the ceremonial kivas. Comforts were added. Various kinds of woven goods were developed: fabrics and ropes and mat-like materials. Clothes and shoes and hats and beds were crafted.

The people of Chaco moved beyond the simple elements of survival. Language was refined. Art developed. Pottery and baskets reflected more than mere function. They painted pictographs to chronicle important events and to record the symbols of culture and mythology. They recorded astronomical observations and invented a calendar.

Clearly, the civilization that grew at Chaco required individuals with specialized skills. Artisans of many types were essential to implement the technologies that evolved: carpenters, masons, weavers, potters, farmers and hunters—perhaps even engineers. And organizers were needed: leaders, spiritualists, teachers, and traders. Individuals became both differentiated from their neighbors and interwoven with them at the same time. The whole needed the individual as much as the individual needed the whole. A new outlook germinated. The individual life glimmered with new meaning, but a humbling sense of connection was essential for survival. The Chacoan people were surrounded by wilderness and more mysteries than answers. Chacoans needed a cohesive sense of community to create so much from the basic ingredients of their environment and the glints of insight scavenged from many trials—and also to forge a fate so dependent upon one another.

And so the lives of the Anasazi in Chaco were connected to the fruits of one another; and connected to their ancestors who gradually accumulated the essential technologies that allowed them to thrive; and connected to the bounty of Earth on which they depended; and connected to cultures beyond the horizon with whom they traded; and connected to a society that required a common vision; and connected to the isolation that protected them. With so many fragile linkages, what must have seemed so solid in its prime was almost certainly destined to crumble and scatter.

As I ride past the great ruins on my way to the campground, I am truly amazed by the scale and precision of the ancient Chacoan people. I am even more impressed by the life they etched from the wild as I strain with my mind's eye to see the sunset as they saw it a thousand years ago—before the sun was seen as a star—looking forward from the past rather than backward from the future.

Tonight, I will sleep not only amongst the coyotes, but also with the ghosts of Anasazi.

**More Day 24:**

I pedaled up to the visitor center at Chaco Canyon about mid-afternoon. The park personnel were quite surprised and quite impressed to see someone rolling into the park on a bicycle. After conferring amongst themselves, they pronounced with certainty that I was the first visitor to their isolated park to arrive by bicycle.

The staff members running the visitor center took an obvious interest in my journey. They advanced lots of tips about the best places to hike and what I should see. One staff member named Paula was especially knowledgeable and helpful. She impressed me with the value of truly loving the work that one does. I reserved a campsite then left the visitor center.

As I biked along the road that followed Chaco Wash, I encountered the ruins. They were right there! They were more obvious than I expected. I couldn't decide if they were larger than I had imagined them or smaller. I had the odd sensation of them being both large and small at the same time. They were right there!

The feeling as I rode past these ruins was very powerful. I felt like I had somehow taken a wrong turn and ended up amongst the ruins of ancient Egypt. Was I expecting heaps of undifferentiated rubble? These were structures—impressive structures with deliberate geometry! This was a lost city! Was it here all this time, just a bicycle ride away? Maybe the graves of Jesse and his companion were guarding a rickety bridge backward in time.

I set up my tent in the campsite and unloaded most of my gear from *Intrepid*. Then I rode back to several of the ruins to walk around them and take some photos. This was much more exciting than I had expected. And I had not set out to come here.

**Day 25:**

I awoke with a renewed sense of purpose and launched quickly to explore the park. There are four main hiking trails in Chaco Canyon. The first one I walked took me to the outlying ruin of Tsin Kletsin, perched atop South Mesa. I was intrigued by the small, outlying developments built on the high places surrounding Chaco Wash. These obviously served some kind of special purpose—but what? The Chacoan people were traders. Were these outposts built to accommodate commerce? Faint traces of a road system radiate away from them. Or were the outposts somehow defensive in nature, built to provide early warning of approaching attackers before they could take up strategic positions overlooking the Chacoan homes inside the wash?

I liked the hike to Tsin Kletsin, not just for the ruin itself, but also for the distant view it provided. Using my compass to guide me in the search, I was able to spot another outpost, Pueblo Alto, on the mesa top across the canyon. It was not difficult to see once I knew exactly where to look. The Anasazi living here and over there would have easily seen each other's fires burning in the night—would have noticed the blink as someone walked in front of the fire—would have realized how a series of winks could send a message instantly across the distance.

I tried to imagine the orange glow of a fire casting outlines on the sandstone walls of Tsin Kletsin late on a crisp autumn evening as Orion broke the eastern horizon. I tried to imagine the flicker of orange across the canyon and the ones scattered along the wash below, all mixing with starlight—the only lights that shone.

I tried to imagine the Anasazi residents sitting upon the rooftops watching a sunset. I had the feeling that misfits were few in this society. Everyone was needed and wanted. Life was so short and mysterious. From where did it come, and where did it go? Sometimes life just seemed to leave and not take the person with it. The value and joy of living must have been obvious to the Anasazi, I imagined. The Earth was as close to them as looking up from their toil. Their neighbors were as close as conversation would carry. And their future was as close as tomorrow. At least, this is how I imagined the Anasazi reality.

With another hint from my compass, I also spotted the ghostly hull of Ship Rock far to the northwest, filtered blue by the great distance.

In the afternoon, I hiked to another outpost named Peñasco Blanco. This trail was especially noteworthy for the many interesting petroglyphs and pictographs along the way, tucked along the walls of the arroyo that led to the ruin. The many chiseled images included coiled snakes, deer and human-like forms with weird proportions and projections. Most impressive was the red-painted picture of a fiery star, crescent moon, and human hand: a trio of images that archeologists believe record the great supernova of 1054 A.D.

*Chacoan record of the supernova of 1054 A.D.*

Some of the petroglyphs were marred by graffiti, a source of great vexation. I do not understand such acts. What degradations of humankind are rooted in the same senseless impulses that lead a person to deface timeless artifacts? I believe that the great atrocities of history and the common violations that happen every day are linked: differing mostly by degree, which tends to increase as the perpetrators get more practice.

Good and evil both exist, along with patterns that are neither. On my journey, I have already encountered the good and the indifferent. I have received many small acts of charity, and I have had one close brush with evil. I am very exposed as I travel, and I hope I do not collide head-on with the latter.

# Day 26:

Once more, I was up and away very early. Chaco had me energized. This time, I hiked to the mesa-top outpost called Pueblo Alto, the one that I had seen in the distance from Tsin Kletsin. From Pueblo Alto, I looked back in the other direction, completing the connection.

The trail continued beyond Pueblo Alto and circled a large basin area with surrounding cliffs and sloping bottom. This basin formed a large, natural funnel for collecting rainwater, a feature recognized and harnessed by the Anasazi for irrigation of crops. The trail also looped past the prehistoric Jackson Staircase, named for its modern discoverer, but which is actually another legacy of the Anasazi. The staircase is a series of steps carved into a cliff creating a connection between the canyon floor and the mesa above. Faint ancient roads cross the mesa and converge at the top of the staircase. In actuality, the staircase looked more like a ladder to me, its slant being almost vertical.

Perhaps the most interesting aspect of this hike was the aerial view it yielded of Pueblo Bonito, the great D-shaped ruin of the largest structure in Chaco Canyon. Pueblo Bonito essentially housed an entire village in a single building—a large village of about a thousand people. Pueblo Bonito was built a little at a time: added onto as needed. It probably started as a curved row of rooms, but adjacent rows, upper levels, porches, plazas and other features were attached over hundreds of years.

The roofs are gone now, and most of the walls are truncated a bit, but the magnificence of the structure at its pinnacle was still easy to imagine. The features that struck me most were the many round kivas, the ceremonial chambers: large, medium and small. The kivas stood out as the round pegs amongst many square holes. Not only did they contrast strikingly, but the kivas also radiated an air of deliberate consideration that resounded across the centuries, even though the builders had long since disappeared.

From the top of the canyon wall, I could see some of the other ruins strung along the floor of the canyon. A question came back to me that first occurred to me as I biked along Chaco Wash, passing the clusters of ruins spaced along a couple of miles of the canyon floor. While the people of Chaco appear to have been comfortable living in large groups close to one another, they still divided themselves into separate villages. Why did they not assemble all of their buildings into one great city? While the villages displayed overall similarities, each village also harbored distinguishing characteristics. Were the Chacoans making lifestyle choices and dividing themselves into neighborhoods of like-minded individuals? Or were there more pragmatic factors that shaped the partitioning of the population into separated units?

Stone-paved roads connected the various villages, and the inhabitants of the different villages cooperated for the general good of the Chacoan state. Also, the people from different villages interacted socially with great kivas being built between villages to provide venues for inter-village events.

I accumulated more questions than answers. I could not solve the mysteries, but I was convinced that many clues about the human spirit lay disguised in the rubble of Chaco Canyon.

*Pueblo Bonito in Chaco Wash*

### Day 27:

Today, Eileen will join me! Yippee! But she wouldn't arrive until the afternoon, so I went on a hike to occupy the morning. I was distracted by thoughts of having company.

When Eileen arrived, we hiked to see some of the petroglyphs along the Peñasco Blanco trail. Then we set up her tent. As the daylight waned, we drove back along Chaco Wash, stopping and walking around the various ruins as we went.

After sunset, Eileen and I grilled hamburgers. She had been kind enough to stop for groceries as she drove from Albuquerque. Of course, she brought me some orange juice.

Eileen also brought me a small backpacking-style candle lantern from Austin. The lantern proved useful for our dinner in the dark and added a cheery glow to the campsite. Eileen also brought my heavier down sleeping bag and my very lightweight down jacket. This jacket was not a serious cold-weather jacket but would give a little more hedge against the cold as I headed into higher elevations and the change of season. Eileen would haul my lighter down sleeping bag back to Austin, along with a couple of other items I didn't seem to be using.

## Day 28:

Eileen explored Chaco from the road while I organized my equipment and took the wheels off *Intrepid* so it could fit into her rental car. Then we hiked to Tsin Kletsin, the outpost on South Mesa I had visited on my first hike in Chaco. We could see Pueblo Alto from Tsin Kletsin, but coal smoke from the Four Corners power plant buried the more distant view to Ship Rock that I glimpsed on my previous hike.

Chaco Canyon was being threatened by energy development, both uranium and coal-fired. No buffer zone protected the park, so energy resources could be mined right up to the park boundary. The seismic activity from such mining could damage the fragile ruins. Outlying archeological sites, as yet undiscovered, probably lay in the paths of mining operations. Some of these outlying sites would hold keys to understanding the greater Chacoan mosaic, keys that might be pulverized in plowing for coal. Once hogged out of the ground, much of the coal was burned in nearby power plants. Besides marring the vistas, the coal smoke also turned the rain acidic, which attacked the ruins and even etched away at the fantastic petroglyphs and pictographs. Water, pumped from deep uranium mines that required dry shafts, was poured into the Rio Chaco, accelerating the erosion in Chaco Wash and threatening to undermine some of the ruins.

We do need power to run our color TV's and air conditioners, but surely some alternatives exist that do not encroach so heavily on the treasures and the mysteries of Chaco.

I left Chaco Canyon riding in Eileen's rental car. We were headed to Mesa Verde for one night. Then Eileen would drop me in Durango and go back home. I would like to have ridden my bike out of Chaco, but I was glad not to face the traffic around Farmington, again.

We stopped in Durango, walked around the historical district, ate Mexican food for dinner, and then drove west to Mesa Verde. We watched the sunset from Park Point, the highest point in Mesa Verde at 8,571 feet. This was Eileen's first trip to Colorado, and she was impressed with the scenery. The campground at Mesa Verde was a large collection of many small campsites, all packed together. This campground definitely lacked ambiance compared to the one at Chaco Canyon. Fortunately, this was not a busy time of year in the park, so we did not feel too claustrophobic in the tight setting. Hot showers were available, and this was enough to cure a lot of other shortcomings.

## Day 29:

Up early, Eileen drove us to the end of the road on Chapin Mesa. We toured Cliff Palace, the largest Anasazi ruin in the park. It tucks into an alcove near the top of a cliff, just over the edge of the mesa. While impressive, the ruins at Mesa Verde have a manicured, museum-like atmosphere to them. They did not affect me as profoundly as the ones in Chaco. Seeing the ruins in Chaco rendered the feeling of discovery. Seeing the ruins in Mesa Verde merely gave me the feeling of being shown exhibits, recreations rather than ancient remains. They weren't recreations, but they seemed like it. The ruins at Mesa Verde would be under great stress were it not for the protection afforded them by the National Park Service, but in some sense, the act of preserving the ruins has also destroyed them.

The physical nature of Mesa Verde itself is quite a bit more spectacular than Chaco Canyon, and the vista alone would be enough to absorb me for hours. As with the ruins at Mule Canyon Wash, I had the impression that the vista mattered to the Anasazi who once lived here and that this location was chosen, in part, for the feelings it generated in them. Perspective—then and now. Although it was still morning and the great vista was mesmerizing, we didn't have time to linger.

# 10. High Passes

**More Day 29:**

Eileen dropped me in Durango and then drove away towards Albuquerque to catch her flight home to Austin. Once again, I adjusted to being alone. The change came as quickly as the thud of a car door. The void was deepened by its suddenness. The effort of filling in where conversation and good company resonated a moment earlier left me a bit shaky and unsettled. I hung around Durango for a while, shopping for groceries, eating ice cream and buying a map. I liked Durango, and it felt comfortable here. If it didn't snow in dump truck loads over much of the year, I could visualize living here. It's beautiful in the summer but no thanks on the snow! As I milled around Durango, my thoughts moved from things just done towards things yet to do. Soon, I had mountains on my mind.

To the north awaited the high passes of the San Juan Mountains, towering as much as a half-mile higher than any pass crossed thus far. Maybe I simmered apprehensively about the next leg of my journey. I did not originally intend to traverse this loop into the high mountains, but I kept covering distances more quickly than I anticipated and adding new detours to my trip. From the start, people asked me where I was headed, and I always answered "California!" Then the same people politely told me I was headed in the wrong direction. Oh, I suppose I have been going the wrong way. High passes or not, my inertia will carry me in the wrong direction for a few more days.

More than just the magnitude of the climbs concerned me about bicycling into the high mountains of Colorado. Despite operating on my own time and my own calendar, the rest of the world had progressed well into September. The weather at the high elevations of the Uncompahgre National Forest could turn vicious soon and suddenly. Days were growing shorter. Moreover, factors beyond the change of seasons could impact me. The brakes on my heavily loaded bike would be challenged. And I was concerned about having a bear or two poke around my campsite while I was trying to sleep. I was not equipped for bear-bagging all of my food and other "smelly stuff."

But I liked the notion of escaping the desert for a few days to an alpine world filled with the scents of big pine and fir trees. And I thought I could equal the task of making the climbs. The possibility of suddenly encountering icy weather still gnawed slightly at my confidence. The decision to go could be dangerous. I wasn't sure how it would work out, but I wanted the test.

I biked northward along US Route 550. Traffic was a bit heavy but not too bad. I was reminded that the area around Durango and Silverton is popular with tourists and was glad to be here with the smaller crowds that visit after Labor Day. Along the way, I encountered one of the coal fired Durango-Silverton trains heading back towards Durango. Many of the tourists sat in open-air cars, tugged along at a pace not much faster than my typical pace on *Intrepid*. A lot of those folks looked tired. Were they worn out or just lulled by the rocking of the train?

I stopped for the night at Purgatory Campground, not quite twenty miles north of Durango. Perhaps four hours of daylight remained, but I did not want to begin the steep uphill climb towards the passes late in the day. I did not know how long the climbs would take, nor did I have a good idea where I might stop between Purgatory and Silverton if darkness overtook me.

Waiting for the night was boring. I didn't come here to sit on a picnic table and wait for the day to end. Compared to what was surely ahead, the view where I was marooned was nice, but not spectacular. I wanted to be near the tops of the mountains, not the bottoms.

## Day 30:

I started early, but I couldn't judge when the dawn actually occurred since it was well hidden by the mountains. The morning broke clear, calm and chilly. I assembled my gear quickly and hopped on *Intrepid* in a flash.

I was gone: past the ski resort, past a few houses and small businesses, then on a gentle trend upward. I swept around a bend to the right and began the real climb.

I shifted down two gears—then another, and another. I think I can; I think I can; I think I can. . . Finally, I alternated between my two lowest gears. Over the course of my trip I had become strong enough to not always need my lowest gear, even on steep grades. I liked the more rapid progress afforded by gear number two, despite the hard work of using it. Compared to the effort of the climb, monotony was the greater challenge because of the long duration of a low-gear pace.

I kept my focus above the pavement rather than looking down to count the orbits of my feet. The view expanded and diversified as I climbed. I cranked into the switchbacks, zigzagging in and out of the reach of the morning sun. As I rounded each turn, I looked backward and outward because the growing panorama behind me was more spectacular than the twisting pavement ahead. From the campground, I was only able to see the forested flanks of the mountains, but as I wound up the curled highway, the horizon assumed the character of a weathered jawbone studded with teeth.

Although the intermittent shadows touched my skin with cold, their chilly fingers could not penetrate the fire that flamed inside me. I wore t-shirt and shorts, as if still in the desert, but felt fine. The coolness outside just balanced the lava heat inside. The thinning air could not deplete me, either. Adrenalin is potent fuel—like rocket fuel, needs no air. For encouragement, I anticipated the top of the climb where the encroaching sky would sharply cleave the upward spiral of the road as the blacktop fell away on the other side.

Traffic was sparse in the early hour. When vehicles did approach, they came in twos and threes. They crept past slowly, but their engines revved high, so they left thick clouds of exhaust in their wakes that did not dissipate quickly in the stillness of the morning. I was thankful there were so few of them.

More quickly than I imagined, I swerved to the left and leveled on top of Coal Bank Pass at 10,650 feet above the Pacific, which was waiting for me in the distance somewhere behind many mountains to the west.

I stayed at the summit for a while but not long enough to get cold. I put on my heavy, long-sleeved shirt and my thin nylon parka along with my helmet to prepare for the frigid descent. I wished I carried gloves other than my open cycling gloves.

The dive down the other side was brief—brakes and hands working hard, leaning into the turns with the inside pedal raised high to avoid scraping the pavement. The cold rush drew tears and stung my exposed hands, legs and face. It was over before the coals inside me could cool.

Then I climbed switchbacks again, this time on the opposite side of the mountain, in the full sunlight. The world transformed into a sea of silver peaks. I felt even stronger. I churned like an engine. I steamed to the top once more—Molas Pass, higher than the first one at 10,910 feet above the distant ocean.

The morning was warmer now, so I lingered at Molas Pass longer than I had at Coal Bank. Then I worked my way towards Silverton, taking my time and stopping frequently to look at the scenery. The highway approached Silverton along the crest of a high ridge and then plunged steeply off the side. I looked almost straight down into the town from high above. The vantage resembled looking down into Silverton from an airplane. I had beaten the train!

After memorizing the scene from above, I plunged into town, swirling down a steep set of switchbacks and crossing the bridge over a swift sparkling creek.

I pushed *Intrepid* around Silverton, exploring the main street and the other nearby streets of the business district, taking careful note of the nature and character of each establishment. I rode all the back streets, spying how the locals lived.

Everything was either old or was made to look old. There was clearly a renaissance in progress but camouflaged to look like the past. A lot of the paint and nails were new. None of the renovations bore the look of high-dollar corporate ventures but appeared more like big dreams by regular people.

The weather was fantastic. Looking straight up into the sky revealed the same kind of dark blue that one would see looking straight down into the middle of an ocean. The aspens were ripe with gold. And I had conquered two very high passes. The day had been good so far, and it wasn't over yet.

I sat on the covered porch of an ice cream parlor drinking vanilla malt, catching up on my log, and starting a letter. Sitting. Thinking. Absorbing. A shady porch in Silverton invites such things, for sure. I understood why folks chose to live here, at least in summer. I still couldn't grasp the attraction of living in the snow. Maybe there's a hidden charm to it. Could someone show me? I'd better not get too enchanted. I still had work to do.

I lifted *Intrepid* from its slumber on the porch and set it back into the sun. I pedaled back across the bridge, swung right onto Route 550 and headed uphill again. I passed several places that I could have camped—but I felt like going.

The upward tilt got steeper—but I felt like going. The day began to slide behind the mountains to the west—but I felt like going. I ran out of good places to camp—so I kept going.

The sky oozed orange and golden hues that signaled the sun had fallen to the real horizon, hidden from me by the peaks all around. I didn't know the distance ahead—but I kept going.

Then I was there, Red Mountain Pass—the highest of them all at 11,018 feet. So, I just stopped.

I finished a great day of riding, perhaps better than I could have imagined: thirty-five miles and three giant passes. But—oh, yeah—I guess the great ride did leave me more than two miles high, in more or less the middle of nowhere. What now?

I knew it would be dark soon. From a distance, I surveyed several open, nearly level areas surrounding a dirt road above the pass. So, I pushed *Intrepid* up the steep dirt road, climbing maybe 150 feet higher than the pass itself, and picked out a level site for my tent with an excellent view down either side of the divide and established my home for the night.

At this altitude, with the sky as clear and dry as it can get, I knew it would be cold that night. Really cold. I was surely glad Eileen had brought my heavier down sleeping bag when she met me at Chaco. I would need every single feather tonight.

## Day 31:

The day started with chanting for warm rays from the sun. Despite pitching my tent high and in the open, the eastern ridgeline eclipsed the climbing sun. The sky blazed overhead, and the peaks to the west were brightly lit. But I lingered in deep shade.

I stayed warm in my sleeping bag, and that amazed me. Whenever it wasn't raining, I left the tent's flap door open while sleeping, zipping only the screen shut so fresh air would flow through the tent and prevent condensation from collecting. A dusting of very cold air sifted through my tent during the night. No frost collected on the inside of the tent, but for the first time on my trip, I detected ice on the outside of the tent—a lot of it. And frost covered the ground, as well.

I postponed getting out of my sleeping bag as long as I could. But soreness crept in from lying on the ground for so many hours, especially in my knees which were not supported by my "shorty" air mattress that extended only from head to thighs. Plus, the voice inside me nagged me not to waste the daylight.

But stepping out into the cold air exposed me to a frigid ambush, as I quickly discovered. The reservoir of heat within me immediately spilled into the cold air and ground, becoming a tiny rivulet in the vast runoff of energy asserted by the Second Law of Thermodynamics. The clothing I carried was simply inadequate for temperature this low, even with the thin down jacket Eileen had brought to me. The air stung the skin on my hands and on my exposed legs. The frozen ground clamped my feet in a vise of pain. My joints locked, and my tensed muscles felt as dead as partially hardened clay. At the moment, what I really wanted from the Second Law of Thermodynamics was for heat from the sun to flow into my cold feet.

I yanked my sleeping bag from my tent, wrapped it around me and half-limped, half-hopped a couple of hundred yards to the sunlight where I danced cautiously in a little circle, turning all sides of me to the warming rays, and padded lightly to restore circulation to my feet. The direct sunlight was little filtered by the crystal air above 11,000 feet, and some relief began to flow into me almost immediately. I was thankful for such a calm morning. A wind would have been unbearable, maybe dangerous.

I ate breakfast while I waited for the sun to reach my campsite. The nearly frozen dried fruit and granola bars were hard and crunchy and required care and effort to eat. I surveyed the area from the lofty vantage point I had earned the evening before. I could see a brilliant red mountain that I assumed gave Red Mountain Pass its name. The colors all around were spectacular: rusted red, silver, brown, and various shades of green, gold and yellow—all brilliant—all set against blue so dark it would border on black were it any darker. But despite its dark tint, the sky overhead contained an obvious energy: a strange union of light and dark.

Red Mountain Pass divides the drainage of Mineral Creek, which pranced beneath the bridge that connected me to Silverton, from the drainage of Red Mountain Creek, which falls to the northeast towards Ouray. From my elevated viewpoint, the cleaving of gravity's dominion into the two basins was dramatically displayed. I could see and hear the volume and momentum of each one gathering in their respective down-slope tumbles. Standing directly above the pass, I lingered in a zone of gravitational indifference where smaller influences acting by chance take rainfall or ice melt a bit to one side of the divide or the other—casting it either north or south along the two different tracks.

Finally, I managed to disassemble my camp and repack the load onto Intrepid. I prepared for the long glide into Ouray. I wore my helmet instead of the usual straw cowboy hat, and I covered my hands with a pair of socks worn over the open bicycling gloves. I was improvising, for sure, but I needed my hands to work well, without cramping, to brake my long and steep descent from the summit. The ride would begin with searing chill, but I encouraged myself with the thought that the air would grow progressively warmer as I rolled down from the heights.

Despite keeping my speed relatively low, the rush of cold air hurt. My nose and ears burned. Behind my sunglasses, tears were ripped from the corners of my eyes, and I had trouble seeing the twisted and occasionally rippled road. The muscles in my hands struggled to apply pressure to the brake levers without knotting in seizure.

I stopped to recover and compose myself at some of the turns dividing the switchbacks. The grade tended to level out on the outside of these turns, and straddling the bike near the cliff-side edges provided the best vistas. If I stopped where the road curved to the right, however, it sometimes meant crossing the road while hoping no vehicle would emerge from around a blind corner. Since traffic was virtually non-existent and the speed of an uphill-aimed vehicle would likely be slow, it was a risk that I was willing to take—cautiously. The views were just too good to not prop myself into the best possible position for scanning.

I suffered mostly around the extremities. My core was still warm. When I stopped, especially in the direct sunlight, the warmth of my core spread outward. I held my hands over my face and blew, trapping the hot air to warm my hands and face.

At the first such stop, I fortified my hands by folding the socks so that a double layer of cotton cloth shielded my grip. This helped.

I kept the cold blasts brief, descending quickly and stopping frequently. I calculated that I was in no real trouble, just a bit uncomfortable provided I stuck to the ritual I was already following. I needed to be patient. It was a beautiful morning, and the thin Colorado air would warm quickly both from the effects of lowering elevation and from the advancing, less oblique heating of the sun.

As I glided down, the worst was behind me. I was okay, and I really enjoyed all of the descent, despite the cold. Like mornings in the desert for which I was better prepared, this morning in the mountains had a special freshness that gets diluted with the wearing of the longer day.

Here and there, small structures were nailed to the steep slopes of the mountains: small, old and improvised—left from the days of starry-eyed prospectors. The scattered ruins had the look of solitary ambitions. How did they choose a place to dig? How many dreams turned to silver, and how many turned to rust? At a prominent switchback where the highway made a bit of a landing before folding backward and downward, I passed an old mill of some kind: larger and more considered with a "corporate" look to it, at least in relative terms.

On my sinuous dive towards Ouray, I felt aware of a sixth sense, not normally considered: a sense of gravity's direction. In this rumpled place, "level" is an uncertain and indistinct quantity. The surrounding forest of uneven peaks steals the horizon, sometimes making up look like down. The slopes cant wildly at many angles, and the road is often tilted like a funhouse floor. Estimates by vision alone are frequently led astray.

In the midst of such a confusing array, balancing upon a heavily loaded bicycle is a dicey proposition, but a subtle sense of the downward vector of gravity seems to direct me to the vertical, keeping me afloat on my bike. In other worlds, sensibly equipped with a stable horizon and orthogonal cues, this sense of gravity perhaps fades into the sensory fuzz. But in this world, tight-roping the road's margin on two skinny tires, this normally hidden sense of gravity seems to steady me like a good hiking stick would on a rocky trail.

I coasted into Ouray having rarely cranked the pedals over the entire distance from Red Mountain Pass. My imagination, however, had been turned a time or two. With the rush of frigid air behind me, I dismounted *Intrepid* at the city's edge and removed the nylon rain parka and thin down jacket, along with the socks covering my hands.

I stayed in Ouray long enough to walk through town and buy orange juice. I walked instead of rode, in part, to give each building a more careful inspection and, in part, because my knees were still too cold to flex easily. Walking produced less pain. Without the novelty of the train, Ouray was less interesting than Silverton. It was more connected to the highway and was more about motels and tourists, around the clock instead of noon to four o'clock. Ouray was okay, with beautiful surroundings and a bit of genuine charm, but there was more façade and less heart to Ouray than Silverton.

I zipped north, following the Uncompahgre River through the tiny town of Ridgway and beyond. The slightly downhill ride was fast and easy, but too many cars and trucks buzzed past me for this part of the ride to be fun. Perhaps I was also decompressing from the exhilaration of the mountains.

Then I turned west on Colorado Route 62, towards the next pass, Dallas Divide. This section of the ride started with some up and down stretches that bobbed past several offbeat houses. These were houses of invention sometimes found along the fringes where a small percentage of people choose to carve homes (sometimes literally): log cabins, domes, A-frames, earthen, and other unusual configurations.

Then the road tilted up, and I began the long and steady climb to the divide. The scattered houses fell behind. This area was more open than the previous parts of my loop through the mountains, with distant views all around. While the mountains ahead and to the south were impressive, this region lacked the color and ruggedness of the alpine corridor from Purgatory to Ouray. This area was, however, more remote and had the peacefulness that comes with isolation. The corridor from Durango to Ouray, more trodden by tourists, assumed an almost gaudy, carnival quality. The Dallas Divide region exuded the feel of being off the beaten track.

The sun beamed intensely, being little diminished by the thin dry air, and it quickly stoked the oven of the day. There was no breeze to evaporate the sweat and, in climbing gear, I generated no breeze of my own. Incredibly, a morning that started so cold morphed into a sizzling afternoon.

Dallas Divide, 8,970 feet above sea level, is a rounded and gradual summit, more subtle than Red Mountain Pass. The summit was scenic and worthy nonetheless, as well as out of the way and hidden. The spectacle of 14,150-foot Mount Sneffels to the south easily justified the ride to the top of the divide.

Peering through distance to Sneffels, the eye bounces up a stair-stepped landscape towards the peak. The eye first skips through the light shades of a wide, gently tilted meadowland that is interrupted by a few scattered stands of aspens and other broad-leafed trees. Then the eye rolls over the tops of a low, rounded set of mountains that form the first step upward to the heights, covered with the darker shades of evergreens. Farther still, the next higher step is a roller-coaster ridgeline, also covered with evergreens. But it is tinged black with the greater distance. Finally, the highest and most distant layer is the blunt, bare face of gray rock: deeply rutted and squinting in the sunlight—rising to a ragged, razor edge with tooth-like Sneffels tearing at the sky.

Silhouetted against the flawless sky, this study of Sneffels stood nothing short of imposing. I tried to imagine the mountain traced against the summer Milky Way: Sagittarius and Scorpius balanced above its highest ledges—a final stepping-stone to greater distances beyond.

Dallas Divide put me at the headwaters of yet another stream, Leopard Creek. I ran downhill along with the Leopard, towards Placerville.

The terrain closed in and assumed a more canyon-like character. I encountered a rising west wind after crossing the divide, and the canyon seemed to funnel and focus the breeze so that it was always directly in my face. Both the slopes and the river valley were densely forested. Aspen leaves of green and gold shimmered and danced in the wind. The road was smooth but narrow, and either rock walls or dense stands of trees blinded many of the curves. I was glad that so few vehicles were using the road.

Where the Leopard leapt into the San Miguel River, Route 62 bumped Colorado Route 145. I veered left onto Route 145 and rode through little Placerville, against the flow of the San Miguel. I cranked past the turnoff to Telluride and climbed southward towards the crests of the San Miguel Mountains. Although it was early, I stopped for the night at Sunshine Campground in the Uncompahgre National Forest. The aspen-shaded campground was deserted. It was lonely here, but beautiful. Pretty meadows stretched to the west and north of the campground, and the pointed peaks of the San Miguel Mountains poked the skyline to the west and southwest. These were impressive mountains that included the "fourteeners" (i.e., mountains with tops in the 14,000-foot range) Wilson Peak and Mount Wilson, both named for the topographer A. D. Wilson who charted this area in 1874.

Close to dark, a small brown pickup pulled into the campground, and its occupants took up residence at the extreme opposite end of the camping area. We never interacted.

The total mileage for the day was 65.1. I could have done more, but Sunshine was a very pleasant layover point.

## Day 32:

The night had not been as cold as the previous one, and the morning warmed more quickly than yesterday's, as well. I was able to strike my tent, stuff my bag, and stow my gear with relative dispatch. The folks in the brown pickup had barely stirred when I pushed *Intrepid* out of the campground and onto the highway.

Sunshine provided scenic but lonely refuge. Clearly, my spirits sagged whenever I halted my ride early in the day, especially in these isolated outposts. The uncertainties of conditions and accommodations that might catch me in the open as darkness falls

sometimes forced me to make early decisions—decisions s ometimes
regretted. My mind seldom stops, seldom slows. It is not good for me
to have time that is not occupied in one way or another.

I cruised in middle gears against a moderate grade for eight miles
to the summit of Lizard Head Pass, which topped out at 10, 250 feet.
To the west, across an expanse of verdant meadow, along a low
ridgeline, stood the chiseled-looking spire that gave the pass its name.

*The solitude and the sloping meadows of Lizard Head Pass*

The gently tilted southern flanks of the meadowland formed a
funnel that collected the first water of the Dolores River. And, as was
often the case at the crest of a pass, the summit marked another
encounter with a mounting headwind.

The Dolores and I rolled to the southwest. Fed by many sharply
defined drainages, the river grew quickly. Fanned by the heat of the day,
the wind also grew quickly. I estimated that the friendly pull of gravity
was just strong enough to cancel out the annoying push of the wind,
making my ride essentially "level."

I stopped at a small store in Rico. The store wore a weathered
exterior and old-looking screen doors. The shelves looked built on-the-
spot, not manufactured and hauled-in. I bought cold orange juice and
dessert, put them into my handlebar bag, and scanned for a lunch stop.

I didn't have to go far. Just before entering town I had crossed an
old bridge that took me over the Dolores. I looped back to this bridge
and found a well-worn path off to one side. I pushed *Intrepid* along the
path to a small, old, metal building that served as a good prop for my
bike. Then I located a comfortable place to sit above the bank of the
river on some kind of wall-like concrete structure that supported some

rusted metal pipes and devices extending down to the water. Maybe this was an old gauging station.

Perhaps kindled by the isolation of this final leg of my loop through the mountains or by the improvised nature of my rest stop, I was overtaken by the same feeling of depth and immersion that caught me on my lunch stop during Day 16 when I pedaled towards Canyonlands. Day 16—that seemed like a long time ago.

I listened to the vigorous rush of the Dolores. She had only trickled this morning before I traced her beginning to her middle with the cranking of my pedals.

At the lunch stop on Day 16, my sight seemed to acquire an extraordinary perception of depth. Today, sound snapped to three-dimensional salute: all of the splashes and gurgles and grinds of the river rushing past me—coming straight to me, as well as echoing from points all around—some splashes approaching, some running away.

I went through the ritual of building my sandwich. Like on Day 16, the flavors were especially distinct, each taste also being woven with the giddy music of the river. The sweetness and chill of the orange juice and tartness of the cherry pie further teased my senses. The here and now enveloped me.

The distinctness of all these stimulations seemed to pry particular moments from the background of blurred memories—moments when paths crossed and then separated. Only the chance meetings at crossroads seemed to matter: the greetings, the short debates, the quick goodbyes, the turned heads, and the last glimpses down the boulevard. The images of those moments at life's crossroads stood out with exaggerated depth, like dolls against a backdrop photo—the dolls casting a shadow onto the backdrop. Only those certain moments seemed real, the rest being stolen from someone else's reality: surely not my own memories since they were so indistinct. Are there only a few fateful moments in life that really matter? I struggled to pull myself from the blurry background of the inconsequential and cast a shadow, making more of my life have meaning—meaning that endured beyond the intersection of two divergent lanes.

I biked on down Route 145, stopping at Forks Campground, situated at the confluence of the Dolores and West Dolores Rivers. A destination for fishermen and families, this campground was much busier than Sunshine. But the campground was large and spread out, with plenty of space between campsites. As I sat on the picnic table at my campsite, I was once again struck by the relative simplicity of my travel. It was simple, yes—but not easy. I conjectured a crossover between simple and complex and between hard and easy that somehow seemed profound. A formula escaped me, however, and I wasn't sure that anyone else would make the connection without doing a trip like mine. Maybe the quality of being profound is also relative.

Once again, I stopped too early. My mind pedaled in place not always taking me to points I wanted to go. The next stop ahead would have been Cortez. I had already ridden through Cortez once on my trip, and I wasn't sure that I wanted to stop there again. Well, maybe I would need to? I didn't have a plan worked out for the next phase of my trip, but I just wasn't in the mood for Cortez today. Cortez reminded me of

Farmington, more function than spirit. It clashed with the turnings in my head. I had been thinking about Barbara all day. I sat on the table and wrote a letter to her. It wasn't enough. I couldn't write enough to put the feeling to rest. I knew it wasn't *all* about her. It was mostly about me, but something about Barbara intensified my feeling.

I was restless, but it was now too late to ride. Patience. Some things need time to unfold.

## Day 33:

The next morning, I cycled into Cortez. Okay—as a matter of logistics, Cortez was strategic. The temperature soared early, and busy little Cortez grew too chaotic and crowded for my comfort. However, I focused on the details of what I needed for my ride, and I handled being in Cortez better today than I could have yesterday. Cortez was actually accommodating for buying supplies and tending maintenance chores.

I found the post office and mailed the letter to Barbara. I bathed *Intrepid* at a carwash. I also needed groceries and film and to patch a couple of inner tubes. The next phase of my trip, I computed, would require an early and flawless start. Despite my attitude, Cortez must be a layover—another "dry docking." So, I secured a motel room and prepared for the long ride to Monument Valley.

# 11. Across the Navajo Nation

## Day 34:

A test of fire awaits me.

I have never ridden a hundred miles. Today, I must traverse the nearly 150 miles from Cortez to the Monument Valley Campground. Although I am now willing to ride across the Navajo Reservation, I have been given enough cautions to discourage me from camping along the highway somewhere in a makeshift bivouac. For at least 125 miles, there will be no refuge and no choice but to somehow go forward. With an early start and no mechanical problems, and a little luck with the headwinds, I think I can make it.

An early start is the key strategy to taming both the wind and the heat since both problems increase with the march of the sun across the sky. I am "on plan" as I cast off from the motel. I awoke before first light, took a shower and ate breakfast, and am on the road by 6:30. I purchased provisions during the previous day's layover. And I repaired, washed, organized and packed my gear while docked in the motel room. Staying inside meant that I did not need to break down and pack a camp this morning.

Cortez slumbers still as I churn out of town. The sun glances low, and the morning is golden and sweet, like honey. The coolness and stillness of the air gives me confidence as I turn south on US Route 666. Gravity leans with me, and the descent to the San Juan River is a fast one: thirty miles in a hurry. Here and there, I chase a roadrunner from the pavement. They look at me as if to say, "What was that?" *Intrepid* is humming and whistling and purring as I throw myself into the ride. I mark miles and see myself advance along the heavy red line on the map. I make the right turn onto the red line of US Route 160.

I did not decide to ride across the large and desolate Navajo reservation in a single, deliberate leap of faith. Paula, the helpful ranger at Chaco Canyon, assured me that I would regret not going to Monument Valley, and she did not think that anyone would harm me. Moreover, the two young cyclists I encountered near Mancos were planning to cross the reservation, and I met an Englishman in the San Juan Mountains who had bicycled on the Navajo lands without problems. So, maybe the people who had given me warnings were well meaning but simply wrong. Could there have been a subtle trace of prejudice in their words of warning? In the final analysis, I decided to cross the Navajo Reservation because I simply couldn't find another way to get from where I was to where I wanted to go.

Mile 38 ushers the Four Corners marker. I stop briefly to watch people take pictures of each other, making ridiculous contortions to simultaneously attach themselves to four different states. Let's see: one hand goes in Colorado, the other hand in New Mexico, and one foot sticks into Utah, while the other foot slides into Arizona. Meanwhile, the bellybutton bobs into Never-Never Land! It's a circus! Between the folks erecting human totem poles over the marker and those busily buying jewelry and curios from the Navajo selling items in carnival-like booths, there is plenty of distraction to obscure the significance of this anchor-point of maps.

*Shiprock*

I turn aside from the midway to survey the perimeter. On this day, the air is really polluted around Four Corners. Mountains barely ten miles distant are diffuse, and a gray curtain hangs beyond them. An interesting view was hopelessly marred by smokestack graffiti from the Four Corners coal-fired power plant that was given a "grandfather" exemption in the Clean Air Act of 1972.

No one else seems to notice, and I don't have time to picket. I can't say for sure that no one else notices, but I listen carefully to the people around me, and I hear no comments about the smoldering perversion that swallowed the horizon.

I fantasize about approaching someone and saying, "Hey, did you notice how dirty the air is way out here in the middle of nowhere? I wonder why that is." I hang around for a few minutes, long enough to decide such an inquiry would be more interruption than conversation. I guess that the lure of the circus is just too strong to allow most people to see.

I leave slightly depressed. Perhaps the difference in my vision is that I must deep-breathe this air to continue my journey.

Just before reaching the spur road to the Four Corners marker, I crossed the bridge over the San Juan River. The ride has not been as easy since leaving the bridge. While the grades were not extreme, the ups-and-downs have been numerous and there has been more up than down.

I am making good progress, over seventy miles by what I judge to be about one o'clock. I passed one meager truck stop, but otherwise the route is essentially deserted. Barely a dozen vehicles hiss and roar passed me each hour. The red line on the map for 160 certainly was not assigned for heavy usage but maybe represents something else.

Then, it happens. A spoke breaks on the rear wheel—freewheel side. The freewheel must be removed.

When the spoke snapped, my reaction was "What the hell was that!" It broke with a loud twang, and the horrendous vibration of the contorted wheel instantly gripped my bike. But I immediately surmise the nature of the cataclysm—very nearly my worst nightmare coming true! As I wrestle *Intrepid* to a stop, I want not to believe what has just occurred. I was lucky that the wheel did not completely collapse in a chain reaction under the heavy load or that I did not crash as my bike shook. But I am now stranded in a dangerous situation with only partial solutions at hand. If only the intensity of my disbelieving stare could weld the broken ends of stainless steel . . .

The freewheel is the ratchet-like device that carries the cogs that drive the rear wheel. It must be removed because it blocks access to the ends of the spokes. I carry a freewheel remover and spare spokes, but I sent the heavy wrench needed to turn the freewheel remover away with Eileen when she met me at Chaco Canyon.

I examine the damage. The spoke parted at a gouge scored when the chain dropped onto the spokes the very first time I shifted to the lowest gear, on the very first day of the trip, caused by the damaged derailleur bracket that was bent by the airline.

Now, I am aground on a desolate stretch of highway: sun high and hot—no trees, no buildings, and no water except what I carry—and no help. I had often wondered if the presence of the asphalt ribbon and the occasional vehicle scurrying past me meant that I was less than alone in this vast desert. As time clicked away, I receive my answer; I am very alone, indeed. The few cars that materialize from the mirages in one direction sail right on past the fallen carcass of the bike and the figure of the rider with broken wheel in hand—then dissolve into the mirages in the opposite direction. Hovering in the dark interiors of the passing vehicles, I can see the reflections of silvered sunglasses swing to stare at the heap on the side of the road. But no one even slows, despite my faint wave and look of desperation.

Okay, this is bad. Okay, I have indeed miscalculated by sending the wrench with Eileen. What was I thinking? Damn! Self-reliance is the number one rule of any endeavor like mine. The fact that I did not need the wrench for the first thirty-three days of the trip did not diminish its significance. Before I started the trip, I packed the weighty wrench because I fully understood that it meant survival, even though I did not expect to use it. Somewhere along the road, I dropped my long-honed understanding of rule number one onto the pavement and rode off without it. Now, I have a real problem.

For over an hour, I try to find a fence post or sign, or something in my equipment that will offer purchase against the freewheel remover. I am having no success and running out of ideas. Perhaps a dozen vehicles pass, with the occupants surely seeing my crippled bike upon the shoulder and the disemboweled wheel—maybe seeing the frustrated expression on my sagging face. No one stops.

Finally, three Navajo riding in an old pickup slow to turn onto a dusty, unmarked side road. They too are going to continue on past me without stopping, but I intercept them before they can drive away— literally standing in front of their truck and blocking their passage on the narrow dirt road. Once halted, they are helpful and polite but show no enthusiasm for the rescue and show no curiosity about the lone stranger on a bike.

They do not have a large wrench but do have a big pair of rusty vise-grip pliers rattling around in the bed of their pickup. They hold my wheel while I adjust the vise-grips and turn the freewheel. Off! Yes! The three Navajo do not wait for me to finish the repair. I thank them, and they are immediately gone without parting words of any sort.

I replace the spoke and true the wheel. An hour and a half have vaporized in the plowing sun. It is now morbidly hot, and the west wind is awake and grumpy. I am halfway to Monument Valley, but over two-thirds of the daylight is gone. The task ahead is daunting, but at least *Intrepid* is working. Besides, there is nothing I can do but ride.

I think about how events on Day 1 have reached forward to shape Day 34. Connections—life always seems to come down to connections.

I can cope with the heat, but the ride now focuses on struggling against the strong headwind. I do not mind pedaling up a mountain because what I put into the climb, I get back on the descent. But working against a headwind is always discouraging because the extra effort expended is just lost since I never reverse direction to catch the tailwind. On this longest of rides, the headwind taunts me more than usual. I try to concentrate on my progress rather than dwell on my losses, but the going is tough. I calculate that I will fall short of my destination unless the wind subsides well before sunset.

As I crest low summits, I can see the long highway taper to the last point on the horizon's sharp edge. I stop for a drink from my canteen on one summit and stare ahead at what seems like an infinite road: narrow and thinning in the distance but sky bright with reflected sunlight, so it is easily traced. I can hear the wavering howl of the wind in the scattered shrub. A feeling of loneliness and isolation passes over me like a crushing wave. I am truly a small droplet in a very large space, trying to resist evaporation.

Eventually, the road tilts slightly downward and lends me energy against the gale. *Intrepid* is humming and singing tenuously, again. At first, the notes are blown off behind me before they can serenade my wilted optimism. But the wind begins to sleep, and the faint but familiar harmony of toiling bicycle parts begins to rise around me.

*Toward Kayenta*

Faster and faster I go. My engine is turned full throttle. Miles click off. The land sprouts and contorts, from an endless sea of monotonous waves to things more interesting, even enchanting, as dark spires of rock poke above the horizon to the north of the highway. Forty-five minutes before sunset I race into Kayenta and then hook right on US Route 163, towards Monument Valley Navajo Tribal Park. Okay, it might almost be dark when I get there, but I will make it.

A mile-and-a-half out of Kayenta another spoke pops with the same dying twang as before—leaving the imploded rear wheel as wrinkled as before. I cannot believe that this is happening. On a day when I need everything to go well, gremlin stowaways planted by the airline have hijacked me twice. Same situation: the freewheel must come off. Same cause: a spoke scored by the chain mishap that resulted from the reckless handling by the airline. I have worked so hard today, and I am so discouraged now.

I hurriedly push *Intrepid* back into Kayenta and find a hardware store minutes before it closes. With some very determined conversation, I convince a clerk in the store to let me borrow a wrench for a few minutes. I quickly remove the back wheel from my bike, attach the freewheel remover, and use the wrench to unscrew the mechanism. I return the wrench to the clerk, and he examines it carefully to see that I have not marred it. Okay, he is visibly annoyed with me, but I really don't care at this point. I politely thank him for his generosity and hustle back to complete the repairs on my bike.

By the time *Intrepid* is fixed, Earth's shadow is rising in the east. There are no obvious options for me to stay in Kayenta, so I begin riding northward—riding hard. Every mile traveled in the fading twilight will certainly be easier than miles traveled after dark. I meter my progress to fuel my determination, but I cannot halt the spinning of Earth, and darkness snares me ten miles up the highway.

For the moment, it quickly gets very dark. Earth has not yet rolled sufficiently upon her eastward shoulder for the rising, almost-full moon to shine over the bordering ridgeline and a distant shelf of high clouds. I can see some glow from the moon along the slender fringes of the clouds, but I cannot see the edges of the road ahead of me. I can only make out the near edge of the road as I look almost straight down upon it. Obviously, I can't ride by looking straight down at the road. And there isn't enough scattered glow for me to clearly see the horizon ahead of me, only the false one to the east, making it difficult to distinguish up from down well enough to securely keep my balance while riding.

Not only has the current day, Day 34, been connected to Day 1 by the mistreatment of my bike by the airline—and connected to Day 29 by sending the wrench away with Eileen—but it is also now connected to Day 29, again, by my decision to detach the generator/headlight from the fork of my bike, also sending it away with Eileen. I had only used the light twice, exiting Salt Lake City on the first night and briefly on the full moonlit night that I approached Lake Powell. I did not really like all the noise that the generator made. I thought I would shed some "unneeded" weight from my load before heading over the towering passes of the San Juan Mountains. Although I had given some calculation to the risk, only now did I fully appreciate my folly.

I retrieve my small flashlight from the side pocket of one pannier. I first try riding while holding it in one hand, but the tiny beam interrupts the dark night so weakly that I am too disoriented to ride safely using just one hand to hold the handlebar. I try gripping the light and the handlebar together but cannot aim the light effectively. So I hold the flashlight in my teeth as I ride onward towards Monument Valley waiting anxiously for the moon to gain the angle needed to light my path.

By the time I reach the turnoff to the park, moonlight has replaced flashlight. But the ride from the highway to the campground is uphill, and I am getting weary. Although the interval was brief, I was worn away by the extra effort of trying to focus the faint flashlight beam on the black roadway by aiming my head. I finally reach the campground and dismount. I lean *Intrepid* against a table; pull out my sleeping bag and air mattress; arrange them on the table; take off my shoes, socks, shorts and shirt; and with some deliberate effort, slither into my sleeping bag. I reckon that my whole body hurts, but I am just too tired to take inventory and determine for sure. And I am too tired to survey the hard-earned surroundings. I have expended virtually all that I can give this day, physically and emotionally. I am amazed that I am here, lying in my feathered cocoon—staring up at the stars that are able to penetrate the growing glare of the low-hanging moon.

I am lost beneath the surface of a deep sleep before I can finish tracing the outlines of a few bright constellations.

Total mileage for the day: 145.9

## Day 35:

I slept solidly. The clear night air chilled deeply, probably cold enough for frost but far too dry. One exchange of equipment with Eileen was proving to be very valuable: the heavier down sleeping bag. I was toasty warm all night despite sleeping in the open.

I awakened once, with the moon high and bright. In the silvery, filtered light bounced into the night from the craggy lunar face, I could see that the campground was perched atop a mesa that inclined rather gently down the flank up which I had ridden. But it was chewed off abruptly in the opposite direction, towards the east. I could see the valley beyond the sharply chopped edge: a significant drop. In the mist of the moonlight, I spied three large buttes rising vertically from the valley floor—long and narrow forms—like three great ships sailing in formation through a glowing fog bank—their tall, sharp bows plowing the desert ocean. Both the size and the relative proximity of these buttes were startling, and their symmetry lent them a sense of grace and motion.

I did not awake again until the sun had nearly risen. I spent some time organizing, eating breakfast, bathing and putting some water back into my body. Indeed, I awoke feeling quite thirsty and still feeling the drain of the previous day's extreme effort. Except for thirst and a little sluggishness, I was not otherwise suffering ill effects from the long ride.

When the ranger station opened, I paid my camping fees and checked into the protocol for visiting the valley. Guided tours were available, but taking one meant leaving my gear unattended. Moreover, taking a guided tour just didn't seem congruent will the nature of my travel. There was also the option of paying an entrance fee and then following a fourteen-mile long dirt road around the valley. But there was one big snag. The road had a great deal of deep sand, and the ranger doubted that I could ride most of the route. After some deliberation, I decided that what I could not ride, I would push. I ended up pushing Intrepid around most of the fourteen mile route. Usually, the sand washed at least several inches deep, making the loaded bike decidedly resistant to rolling. And some of the sand was deep enough to even make walking difficult. However, the fantastic spires, buttes and cliffs all around made the push easily worth the effort.

Monument Valley is not only a park but is also home to many Navajo families. Occasionally as I pushed, I would encounter Navajo or their dogs—sometimes both together—also walking the road. They would appear out of nowhere, materializing from somewhere off the road, then vanish from the roadway behind me. Here and there, I spotted hogans, traditional homes of the Navajo fashioned from materials taken from the earth nearby. A few times, Navajo residents drove past me in pickup trucks, as did groups in guided tour vehicles. The vehicles left big, disagreeable dust clouds in their wake. So, I was very pleased that such encounters were infrequent.

I completed my trek around the valley early in the afternoon and stopped back at the visitor center before heading to the campground. I was now accumulating enough encounters with the Navajo to get some general sense of them, at least in regard to how they interacted with me. There is danger in making sweeping extrapolations, but I noticed a very pronounced pattern of behavior. The Navajo were not hostile, but neither were they friendly. They always shared the road but never showed a spark of interest in a lone bicyclist trying to cross an awfully big desert. If I said "Hello," which I always did, many Navajo acted as if they had not heard me. All would politely answer direct questions, but none would make conversation.

Their eyes would not follow my movements. Their focus would be on the wall beyond me like I was invisible to them. If I waved, I counted one in four would wave back to me. If I gave a cheerful greeting, only one in three would respond. Even the Navajo that appeared along the road in the middle of nowhere totally ignored me as resolutely as those who were standing around a store. Navajo children *would* notice me, even smile at me or give a little wave. If a parent observed the child doing this, the parent would immediately interrupt and distract the child, often pointing and directing the child's attention somewhere else.

I sensed an ember heated by the many, many years of friction between the Navajo and the "white man." It wasn't a flame—just a glowing ember.

I was saddened by this realization, although not surprised by it. But the actual experience of bumping into this barrier was profoundly disconcerting to me. Both the Navajo and the "white man" have lost something in this breach.

I know that the Navajo love this land. I do, too.

Back at my campsite, I needed to prepare for the long ride across the remainder of the Navajo nation. Mostly, this meant giving some additional attention to the troublesome rear wheel of my bicycle.

Bicycle wheels are curious contraptions that combine many flexible wire spokes into a rigid unit. The strength of the wheel depends upon the tension, or pulling force, in the spokes. For the wheels to be sufficiently strong the tension in the spokes must be very high—soprano high when plucked like a harp.

The circular rim of the wheel opposes the tension of the many spokes that are laced within its arc. So, the rim itself must be quite strong to resist collapsing under the inward tug of the spokes. But the strength of the rim depends mostly on its geometry. It must be straight, as in divided evenly by a plane: not wavy from side to side. If the rim becomes curled a little bit, away from the straight and planar, it will be hopelessly crushed into a pretzel-like bend by the huge forces applied to it by the spokes.

The spokes are angled outward a little bit as they pass from the rim to the hub (at the center of the wheel). This small angle means that the spokes pull the rim a little to the side as well as pulling towards the hub. On a spiffy, straight wheel, there are as many spokes pulling a little to one side as there are pulling to the other side. So, the pulling to each side is balanced by the pulling to the other side, and the rim stays straight. In fact, this balanced side to side pulling by the spokes is essential for the wheel to have any side to side strength.

When a spoke breaks, the side to side pulling becomes unbalanced, and the wheel deforms. And as it does, the tension in the remaining spokes redistributes so that the total pull of the spokes against each other, along with the tugs added by the distorted rim itself, all balance out. In the crumpled wheel, some spokes have more tension than others.

When I replaced the two broken spokes, I tightened each of the new spokes enough to make the rim straight again. But this adjustment alone did not guarantee that the tension in all the spokes was the same, once again. The rim and the old spokes were not likely to return exactly to their former condition. When some spokes are left pulling harder than other spokes, the ones pulling hardest are more likely to break.

I needed to "play" each spoke, listening to the tone it made, and then adjust the tension in spoke after spoke until all the spokes would play the same note—having the same amount of tension in them. However, adjusting the tension in a spoke changes the shape of the rim, producing a side-to-side wobble whenever the forces on each side of the rim are not balanced. So, adjusting the spokes is a process that involves both shaping the wheel, eliminating side to side wobbles and eccentricities, while evening the tension in all the spokes. It's an iterative process with many cycles of repetition.

I spent more than two hours truing the rear wheel. And I inspected the other spokes for damage. The two spokes that broke had been scored by links in the chain when the chain dropped off of the largest cog on the first day of my ride. The score marks concentrated stresses, which caused the spokes to fatigue at those two points.

When a bicycle wheel rolls along, the ground pushes up on the tire and rim causing the tension in the spoke at the bottom of the wheel to decrease slightly. As the wheel turns, each spoke rotates to the bottom position and has its tension momentarily decreased. Then the spoke's full tension is restored as it rotates away from the bottom. Thus, each spoke goes through many cycles of increasing and decreasing tension that tend to fatigue the metal over time. For an undamaged spoke, the number of cycles required for the spoke to fail is enormous, probably more than can be counted in a lifetime of riding. But the concentration of stresses along a score mark greatly reduces the number of stress cycles required before the spoke fails.

A couple of the remaining spokes have very light score marks on them, but these scores are not nearly as deep as the ones on the two

spokes that failed. With the tension in the spokes now evenly distributed, my guess (or hope) is that none of the remaining spokes will
give way. But I am a little nervous—and my tension is a little less
evenly distributed.

I sit on top of the picnic table at my campsite, feet propped on top
of the bench, having a cold drink snared from the vending machine and
studying the horizon. The campground's position at the edge of the
high mesa lends it a fine view in several directions. The temptation is to
get caught up in the majesty of the valley itself and not let the eyes
walk to the horizon. But there is a longer view to scan.

There it is again—off in the hazy blue distance to the northeast—
Comb Ridge!

It had first captured my attention, anonymously, out the window of
the airplane. Then I saw it in the distance from the high country
outside Natural Bridges. A couple of hours later, I stood at its base,
looking up at its sheer face and the ominous grade that slashed
across it. Then I rode over its wavy top, and along its less fearsome-
looking backside. I thought that I had left it behind in Blanding, where
the old gentleman in the motorhome quizzed me while I fixed a flat tire.

But there it is: its convoluted spine quite unmistakable. I am
connected again after my long, twisted loop into Colorado and New
Mexico—here to there—where I am to where I was, way off in the fuzzy
distance on my bicycle.

## Day 36:

Before dark, I added the miles on the map: Monument Valley to
Sunset Crater, more than160—a long ride. As I dissolved into sleep, I
had set the clock in my head. Now, the alarm sounded. I clicked instantly awake, fully awake and moving purposefully.

When my mental alarm sounded, Earth had spun just enough to
allow a trace of sunlight to faintly scatter in the high atmosphere
visible low over the eastern horizon. Not enough illumination had
gathered to call it "first light" over Monument Valley. Perhaps it was
first light over Cortez where I had been one bike ride earlier. Maybe it
was the high atmosphere overhead there that was now catching the
first direct rays of sunlight: up high enough to barely peek over my
horizon here.

At Monument Valley, the stars were still shining. The winter constellations of Orion, Taurus, Auriga and Gemini circled overhead as I slept, standing where Cygnus, Lyra and Aquila had been when my eyes winked shut. Earth's dancing partner, Moon, had glissaded from horizon to horizon, and now looks back with her slightly turned face as she exits the stage to the west.

Orion, flying near the meridian before dawn, gave me warning that the season for my bicycle odyssey would be ending. Earth, which seems so immense and unyielding, has been silently weaving in a gravitational pas de deux with the Moon, each leaning in balance away from the other as they whirl together along a great ellipse bent around the sun— together moving about 1,100 miles along their shared orbit in the time it takes me to turn the crank on my bicycle in sixty little circles.

In the predawn hour of Orion, I ride on Earth's front bumper. Monument Valley is turned into the direction of Earth's flight, the air above ramming space—sweeping up more meteors before the dawn than it did after dusk when Monument Valley rode on Earth's tailgate.

I hurriedly disassemble my camp and secure the equipment: sleeping bag and tent onto the rack, and the ground tarp and air mattress into a pannier. As I mount *Intrepid*, I can see the silhouettes of the three prominent buttes anchored beyond the cliffs at the edge of the campground, outlined against the rapidly growing glow that will become the day. A few dozen of the brightest stars remain visible as I take a last scan of the heavens before turning my attention to the pavement.

The air is clear and dry but heavily weighted with a near-freezing chill. On the downhill glide from the campground to the highway, the slicing cold punctures my exposed skin. I pause at the bottom of the grade to retrieve my spare socks to cover my hands. Only the morning at Red Mountain Pass was colder than this one. I try to ride, but my knees seize and grind. I will have to warm them, gradually bending them more as they thaw. I escort *Intrepid* along the shoulder in a slow, stiff-legged shuffle at first—then with cautious flexing of the joints, increasing the amplitude little by little.

Sirius is now the only star I can find, and it quickly fades into the bottomless tide of blue. Within a few minutes, the modest star to which Earth is invisibly bound becomes a constellation of one that rules the sky. Earth's shadow has set in the west. Only the solitary pirouette of the slightly waned moon still stands in defiance.

With the horizon now rotated below the sun, I test the saddle and ride in a low gear, then a little higher gear and another. I am warming from within, although the air is still cold enough to singe my face and ears. I do not need to use the brakes, so I tuck my hands in behind the handlebar bag to shield them against ramming the air ahead. The oblique, yellow fingers of sunlight tickle my skin wherever they can reach it.

Except for my willowy wake, the air drapes in perfect calm. The symphony of thin spokes, narrow tires, pulling chain, and splitting air build around me. Once again, I am an engine with throttle open. All too soon, I am blasting through warm rather than cool air, and the heat of my engine is spreading throughout me. I pause to peel the extra layers of clothing and swallow some tea. It never ceases to surprise me how quickly the sun engages the thin, dry air of a high desert—or how quickly that grip is lost after dark. I can already tell that the real challenge of the day will be staying cool, not keeping warm.

By the time Earth has turned enough to make my shadow less than the width of the road, I have churned the twenty-five miles back to Kayenta. I lean right, ignoring the stop sign at the empty highway junction, swinging back onto US Route 160. I head west again on roadway that I have not yet tested—towards Grand Canyon.

It is seventy miles to Tuba City, the next town on the map.

The ghostly spires and buttes of Monument Valley and Kayenta give way to a less sculptured land of long mesas and broad rolling valleys. For a few miles, I am riding parallel to a creek but against its flow. Throngs of majestic trees line the creek and stand in bold contrast to the red sandstone walls behind them.

Then I enter a more open desert land with long steady grades: angled a little up, then a little down—over and over.

I am looking for the changes in the land that will transform it from monotonous desert into the enchanted plateaus that surround the Grand Canyon. At this point, the transformation eludes me. The trend doesn't seem to go from here to there. Somewhere ahead, a discontinuity must be crouching.

The day now bakes, but fortunately the wind is napping lazily. I search for a patient rhythm to take me to Tuba City, still more than fifty miles ahead. I have time to think—time to integrate—time to listen to the voice inside—time to explore with the mind's eye.

Time has changed. It is now connected to my shadow instead of a watch. Days are connected to the count in my journal instead of a calendar. The season is connected to the position of the sun against the background of constellations instead of the backdrop of rituals and routines. I am entangled with the vivid sensation that the swing of my shadow and the spin of the earth and its loops around the sun all measure me—my time to spark in the dark. Life is ephemeral and can be gone before you even notice that you have one.

I pass an area known as Black Mesa where coal is mined for the Navajo Power Plant near Page, Arizona. To my right, the rail tracks built to transport the coal straddle a ceaseless ridge-like bed, piled up to create a level passage for the coal trains. Sometimes the highway and railway are very close, and the piled-up rail bed blocks my view of the northern horizon. When the highway and the railway diverge a bit, I can see the high rounded top of Navajo Mountain, forty miles to the north. The terrain close at hand is much less inspiring.

As hard as I try not to, I sometimes lose the connection to the feeling of freewheeling in the wide-open West. I have to mentally pinch myself. "I'm really here!" When the connection breaks, I seem reduced to being a character in a dream that jumps suddenly from point to point, then backtracks and makes exactly the same jerky jumps. My journey is chopped into a photo album without a story, leafed through again and again.

The highway bends more to the south where the railway turns more to the north. For a moment I can see down its length, the two rails coming closer in the distance but never quite touching. The rails go their way, and I go mine—twenty-eight more miles to Tuba City.

Sometimes, I feel that I am on a mission—holding my breath and diving beneath the surface to swim out of a whirlpool dream. In these moments, I sense that I am converging upon some unknown but important quantity.

I pedal up a steep hill to the small Hopi village of Red Lake, tucked away in the chopped-off northwest corner of the Hopi Indian Reservation that just touches the highway for a few miles. Nothing looks inviting. Nothing stirs, not even a dog. I don't break my cadence as I continue over the hill—twenty-one more miles to Tuba City.

I believe that my father swirled away much of his life in the undertow of a dream. He fought for General Patton in the Second World

War. He knew about life and death. He surely felt the urgency. But expectations, hard-luck and the inertia of commitments kept him locked in the eddy.

He died too young, at fifty-five. And he died with regrets.

My mother and father were divorced when I was sixteen. It was sudden. I'm not sure he saw it coming.

I did not see him again for ten years—a few stilted words on the phone now and then—but nothing more until he was dying. I never allowed myself to think about his loneliness, and he never tried to contact me.

The hills roll by like waves flattening themselves upon a beach. My legs feel so strong—I can do this forever. Fifteen miles to Tuba City.

When I learned of his illness, I visited him several times in the hospital. He talked a little about the wilds of Idaho where I was born. He spoke simply of incomprehensible forces that make life go on. He was trying to live, but he knew he was dying.

At fifty-five, he was planning to retire early. He bought a new van and was going to outfit it for camping and long travel. At fifty-five, he was finally going to have some fun—finally tinker a few dreams into reality.

At fifty-five, he died of a rare form of leukemia that didn't exist before we invented so many insidious poisons.

He was the next to youngest of ten. He was the next to first to die. His siblings gave him a sparse funeral—said nothing in his behalf—said nothing to my sister and me. I felt like an intruder at his funeral. I didn't hear much of the made-for-hire eulogy by a minister who had never met him.

Faster—faster I go. Uphill—downhill, *Intrepid* sings a gathering soprano, never pausing to inhale. Twelve miles to Tuba City.

After the service, some of his friends from work approached my sister and me and told us how he had often spoken of us—proudly spoken of us. They had taken up a collection and wanted to know to what charity it should go.

Mostly, they came to tell us that our father was a good yet misunderstood man who had loved us from a distance.

Where do the chances go? In the hospital, it was very difficult for me just to hold his hand. It is so strange to leave a place without someone because they no longer exist—except in memory. And mine had holes.

Life is played for keeps. Sometimes we are fortunate enough to carry the baton lost by another—if only we realize it.

Off eight miles ahead, I can see reflections from metal roofs. My shadow is still short, but is growing longer and angles off to the east. Legs like pistons, I soon burn into Tuba City. The fire inside me is very strong today. I stop briefly for a cold drink and then swoop down the grade towards the junction with US Route 89.

I sprint to the edge of the discontinuity that separates the spires and buttes of the Navajo lands from the high realm of the Grand Canyon. I begin to see the transformation I have been trying to imagine. The level earth falls away to a fractured bottom. Higher worlds rise abruptly from its far perimeter. First, I see the hazy distant outline of Humphrey's Peak. Then, I spot the Kaibab Plateau. Finally, as I descend the steep drop to the highway junction, over my right shoulder I spy the pink and purple bands of the Echo Cliffs. I have entered the neighborhood of the Grand Canyon, only one desert basin ahead, but my path there will not be straight.

*Off in the fog of distance. . . Humphrey's Peak*

I swing left, crossing the lanes of Route 89. A heavy red line marks this highway on my map. There is more tourist traffic along this route, and the Indians have set up souvenir booths at the highway junction. Vehicles practically crash into each other as drivers make hasty maneuvers to pull over to the booths. The scene seems surreal and disorienting to me, and I have to weave and bob to avoid being hit by the rush to buy trinkets. Is there a hidden camera? It seems like a joke.

I push south, quickly covering the fifteen miles to the canyon of the Little Colorado River. I stop at the bridge. Next to it is an old suspension bridge, now closed to anything except foot-traffic. The old bridge is interesting, and I imagine a connection to a time when this was still a frontier. The gorge below the bridge would be impressive in another setting. But here, it is a mere tease hinting at what lies not too far beyond.

The bridge marks the low point for the day's ride. All the area to my east, the direction from which I have descended, drains beneath the two bridges. The roadway at this point is about 4,000 feet above the distant Sea of Cortez, where the water of the Colorado is destined but will never arrive. The remainder of my ride to Sunset Crater will be spent climbing up from here, to around 7,300 feet. My anchorage is still forty miles in front of me.

I pedal a few hundred yards to the large "trading post" at Cameron. This is a tourist stop that could star in any movie that required one. If filming a comedy here, all that would be needed would be to set up the camera. No script would be required. The fuss over cheap plastic trinkets astonishes me. The bickering between family members is also astonishing. The surrounding landscape is salted with fascinating, although subtle, detail—but very few people are taking the time to look around at it—to sense it in a way that cannot be done from the interior of a vehicle. The voices around me are loud and tense—and some are even demanding or angry. Many people come here, but very few ever are here. To me, the chaotic activity rings with comedy of the absurd. Clearly, I have cycled into a realm inhabited by a different brand of "tourist" than I encountered along the remote sections of my route. But there is a large covered porch with plenty of cool shade and cold drinks and ice cream inside. I go in for both.

Gone are the curious questions and inspections of my bike. Although I bathe daily, people walk in wide circles around me. They pause to let me pass or stand out of my way to let me go first. They avoid looking me in the eye, using only the corner of their own. No one goes near *Intrepid*. I have not had this reaction elsewhere, so I assume I have merely ventured beyond my natural domain. I miss the friendly rural stores of Utah and the guys traveling in motorhomes with a pair of

Schwinns tied to the back that would ask me how far I've come. I am fairly sure that none of the souvenir seekers here would help me if I needed it.

The "trinket tourists" don't seem happy to be here and are mostly oblivious to their surroundings other than the fact that it's hot and a long ways between restaurants. Why do they come? They busy themselves collecting enough junk to prove that they were really here and then head home to impress neighbors with their "adventure," even though they probably never leave the air conditioning for more than half an hour during their entire trip. I'm sure the trinket tourists represent a small fraction of visitors to the Grand Canyon, but they must be attracted to particular watering holes, and this is one of them. Were I traveling in a vehicle, I'm sure that I would have instinctively passed this zoo. On a bike, it was shade and a cold drink, so I stopped.

I cannot dwell on this longer. I still have much more work to do today. I finish an ice cream bar, soft drink, and an orange juice chaser—then ride onward.

As I climb to the south, I glance back over my shoulder towards the Little Colorado. I look for the dark snaking shadow that might mark the top of its gorge. I try to visualize the Little Colorado's course to the confluence with the mightier Colorado, trying to calculate where the smaller river first carves into the highlands of the Kaibab Plateau. Mostly, its path remains a mystery to me. Here and there I think I see its way, but connecting the dots is more about imagination than what I can actually see.

I wonder about different realities. Some seem shallow to me, but all are a delicate balance. Reality is a lot like a bicycle wheel. It seems rigid and definite but is made from a bunch of spindly, flexible things laced together with opposing tension, adjusted to make the rim of reality roll more or less straight. Some of the spindly spokes of reality are natural and some are inventions. Different people lace these elements in different proportions and with different tautness. Different realities, like different wheels, give different rides. However mixed and however tightly strung, when a spoke breaks, the reality crumples. Sometimes, inserting a new spoke is not enough. Sometimes, one must build a new wheel.

And like a spoked bicycle wheel, reality depends on geometry: the shapes and sizes of the components and the pattern of the lacing. For me, there is relevance in the natural order of the physical world and the patterns in the weave. Some realities are more valid than others because there is more geometry in them. There's a lot of geometry unfolded in this place.

By sunset, I have covered 143 miles. By dark, I have covered twelve more. At this high elevation and under clear skies, the night is cooling rapidly. My knees begin to feel the wear and tear of three hard days as they absorb the cold.

There is a white line along the edge of the highway that I can follow in the darkness. But my balance is slightly shaky in the low climbing gear, and it is worsened by limited visual references. Although Scorpius is mostly gone, Sagittarius and much of the dense surrounding summer Milky Way pours down to where the pavement meets the sky, providing a faint horizon. But my eyes get spun around in the darkness as I try to scan from white highway stripe to the black line cutting off the star clouds that marks an ethereal horizon. The headlights of occasional passing vehicles provide some temporary illumination, but they also blind my night vision for a few minutes. I try a method of one eye open and one eye shut when vehicles approach. It is all very precarious.

I could wait for the Moon to rise, but I am getting sleepy, as well. I push on.

Finally, I reach the turnoff to the national monument campground. It is too dark to stay afloat on this road. I dismount and walk *Intrepid*. But I am close, now. I pass the marker at the monument entrance. I am getting weary, sleepy, and stiff. Not much further to go. As I walk into the campground, shafts of moonlight stab obliquely through the trees.

I lean *Intrepid* against a concrete picnic table. I sit on top of the table in my usual pose, feet resting on the bench. I can hardly believe that I've made it here, 162.4 miles from where I started the day. I have now covered 1,556 miles on my trip—322 of those miles in the last three days while crossing the Navajo Nation.

I take several minutes to collect myself enough to move again, this time just to retrieve my air mattress and sleeping bag. With difficulty, I muster the effort to inflate the air mattress, unpack the sleeping bag, and stretch them out on the tabletop. My right knee really hurts now. I shape a pillow from the stuff sack and some of my clothes. I crawl painfully into the bag and lay my head on the makeshift pillow.

Then I am gone.

# 12. Dancing in the Desert Night

## Day 37:

Hmmm. I think I've figured this one out. A concrete picnic table makes a cold, hard bed. By morning, my body was stiff and sore, especially my right knee. I was able to sleep through the night simply because I was too exhausted to be aware of the pain.

By the time sunlight poked through the trees creating a makeshift camouflage around me, the unyielding table was inflicting more punishment on me than the previous day's long ride. It made too hard a bed for a morgue. I wished for some help shedding my sleeping bag and sitting upright on the table. I knew I would not be going far today.

I also quickly realized I didn't have the slightest semblance of a plan. Maybe I wouldn't be going *anywhere* today.

I sat for a few minutes, just trying to wake up fully. Then I tried putting on my shoes. The stiffness would go away with movement, but my right knee was really sore. The knee needed rest.

I hiked a little to help work out the soreness that extended virtually the length of my body. I walked slowly and with a bit of a limp, trying to minimize the stress on my lame knee. Mostly, I watched the squirrels and the blue jays patrol the campground.

Sunset Crater is a volcanic cinder cone. It's not very old, in geologic time, and the Anasazi living in the area witnessed its formation only a decade after the great supernova of 1054 A.D. There must have been some interesting philosophical discussions in the kivas during that time with all the big explosions going on.

When I was in the eighth grade, my science teacher recounted the sudden formation of a volcano in a cornfield on a Mexican farm. According to her rendition, this was just an ordinary cornfield until, one day, the ground just split open without warning, and a volcanic cone started growing very rapidly. I found this account to be both shocking and fascinating. I wanted to watch an event just like it. I kept watching all the fields around my neighborhood, hoping intently for an encore within easy pedaling distance from home.

Well, the Anasazi who once dwelled in a nearby village, the ruins of which are called Wupatki by the Hopi, lived my daydream. Without warning, the volcano that explorer John Wesley Powell named Sunset Crater popped up in their cornfield. Of course, the Anasazi of Wupatki were smart enough to flee the explosive eruption, but I probably would have stayed to watch.

Powell named the cinder cone for its striking red coloration derived from the iron in the cinders. Iron is an interesting element. Not only is it essential for human life and the frames of tall buildings, it is the most stable of atomic nuclei and the heaviest element forged in the crucibles at the cores of normal stars.

Stars make a living by fusing lighter elements into heavier ones with the reactions liberating energy that flows outward into space. The process begins with stars making helium from hydrogen. Hydrogen is the lightest of all elements and is also the most abundant element in the universe, accounting for about three-fourths of all material. Almost all hydrogen originated within a few minutes of the birth of the universe. Helium is the second lightest and the second most abundant element, contributing about one-fourth of the substance in the universe. Like hydrogen, most helium is primordial and was distilled in the first moments of existence. It is staggering to realize that our world, including our bodies, is partially woven with material that dates to the beginning of time. Scale.

But some helium is not primordial and was forged more recently by the nuclear reactions at the cores of stars. Stars spend the bulk of their energy producing lives carrying out the hydrogen-to-helium cycle. This is the reaction that fires the sun in its current state of evolution. When a star depletes the supply of hydrogen at its core, it begins fusing helium into still heavier stuff. Eventually, elements like calcium, carbon, oxygen and nitrogen—the Tinker Toys in the chemistry of life—are all built up by one sequence or another in the nuclear furnaces at the centers of stars.

In each case, when two lighter elements are fused into a heavier one, energy is released. But the sequence ends with iron. Iron is the bottom of the nuclear energy well. Outside energy has to be put into a reaction to build an element heavier than iron instead of the reaction releasing energy. Thus, a star making anything heavier than iron would have to *absorb* huge amounts of energy *from* the surrounding space— rather than *releasing* energy *into* space.

Elements heavier than iron are assembled from the maelstrom of energy in the explosions of supernovae like the one the Anasazi witnessed in 1054 A.D. Massive elements such as gold or uranium gradually decay, slowly releasing the extra energy temporarily borrowed from an exploding star. So elements heavier than iron trickle towards the iron bottom of the energy well. But the backwards slide towards lighter elements must stop at iron because splitting iron into lighter elements requires replacing the energy that was poured into space by a star as it constructed iron from lighter elements. As a rule, Nature favors minimums— especially energy minimums.

In total, elements heavier than helium account for only about one percent of the material in the universe. The amazing thing to ponder from the table top in my campsite is that enough iron has found its way from the cores of dead stars to this waypoint outside Flagstaff to ruddy a mountain-sized cinder cone. It is also amazing to consider how enough scarce nuclear ash collected in one lonely outpost called Earth to incubate the bounty of life upon her. Nature does not fill the vacuum uniformly—but tucks little lockets, scattered here and there, with rare bits of her potions and then waits patiently for magic to develop. Perspective.

I was quite concerned that I might be stuck at Sunset Crater for several days while my knee healed or that the soreness might be aggravated every time I continued with my trip. Would Sunset Crater or nearby Flagstaff be the end of the ride?

I walked to the visitor center to call Eileen. She had mentioned she might want to connect with me at the Grand Canyon. Indeed, the call confirmed she was still interested in meeting me there along with a mutual friend, Nancy. But it would be about two weeks before they could come.

I anticipated an extended stay at the Grand Canyon, but I didn't want to wait in one location for so long. I would need to add another loop of some sort to my ride. I sat on a picnic table studying my map, looking for a potential route. A loop extending south of Flagstaff and past Sedona could be fashioned by connecting several sections of highway with smaller gray-line roads. Some of the loop extended through desert terrain, and some of it was forested. The map did not indicate any campgrounds for a large section of the loop along the southern reach. I didn't like that. But overall, the loop looked interesting.

I pitched my tent in hopes of having a softer and warmer night of sleep. Then I settled on the table again and wrote a long letter to Barbara, including a number of excerpts from my journal. Sitting in one spot wore upon my mind even though my body was getting needed rest. It was a balancing act.

I didn't think I could sit another day. The knee must be ready to ride by morning.

## Day 38:

My eyes open, and I move from sleep to fully awake in the same quick motion. Instantly, I focus on my right knee. There is no pain. I roll over and move the leg a bit, straightening and flexing the knee very cautiously. There is no pain. I crawl out of the tent, stand up, and take a few careful steps. There is no pain. I strike my tent, stuff my sleeping bag and pack my gear. I'm ready to ride.

I actually start out by walking *Intrepid* for maybe a half-mile just to make sure that my knee is warmed and ready to go. Then I ride slowly in a medium gear. Thankfully, I do not have to start out the day with a climb. The pedaling is easy, and the knee is taking it well. But I decide not to push my luck and will try to avoid stressing the knee very much, at least for today. Nature, after all, favors minimums.

The morning is beautiful, with tall dark green pine trees thrusting into the indigo sky. Optimism reigns. I head towards Flagstaff, only twenty miles away. Not far down the road, I come to a KOA and stop for a shower. Armed with a clean body, a perfect day and fresh optimism, I pump the rest of the way into town, ready to have some fun. Not even the city traffic is able to dampen my light-hearted mood. I'm feeling pretty good.

When I get to the old downtown, I abandon the pavement to walk my bike along the uneven sidewalk that charts the evolution of the business district with changes in the concrete: little ups and downs, and variations in color, texture and width. The nearly 7,000- foot elevation of Flagstaff keeps the morning pleasantly cool. Most of the shops have their front doors open, inviting in both cool air and customers. Here and there, I lean *Intrepid* at a window of a shop and go inside. I look at books about the region; ponder the virtues of getting a new canteen; wonder if I will need gloves again. I finally buy a chocolate brownie at a small bakery. I learn that the old Lowell Observatory on Mars Hill at the edge of town has a public tour just after lunch. I decide to go.

I thread my way to the western side of town, making a few turns that don't end up taking me where I need to go. I can see what I believe to be Mars Hill, but I don't have a city map. That's okay. What I do have is some time for exploring since I am early for the tour. Eventually, I find the large city park that borders the observatory, and then I find the steep road to the top of the hill. I make a patient, low-gear climb to the pine-forested summit. The knee is fine.

At the top, I see the newer brick administration building and the old white-painted wooden structure (not really a dome) that houses Percival Lowell's old telescope. The observatory grounds have a deceptive "off in the mountains" feel to them. It's hard to believe that I am only a few minutes ride from the city's edge. Squirrels and blue jays chatter and squawk at me as I build a sandwich and wait for the tour.

The Lowell Observatory is perhaps best known for the discovery of Pluto by Clyde Tombaugh in 1930. But it is Lowell's own pursuit of Mars that gives the observatory its most colorful history. Lowell was born to a wealthy Bostonian family and was a Harvard-educated mathematician.

After drifting a bit, he developed a passion for astronomy and an especially keen interest in the planet Mars.

Really an amateur astronomer with extraordinary means, he embarked upon the mission of building an extraordinary observatory for engaging his new hobby. He purchased a twenty-four inch refracting telescope from fellow Bostonian and world-renowned telescope builder, Alvin Clark. Among the world's largest telescopes when it was purchased in 1896, Percival had the thirty-two foot long behemoth transported to Flagstaff by rail. A small group of local workers fashioned the odd, flat-topped, tapered-sided "dome" from planks split from Ponderosa Pine taken around the observatory site.

Percival Lowell spent many nights looking through his giant glass at the magnified, but still tiny, disc of Mars. He was intrigued by the notion that there were canals on Mars, built by an ancient civilization to carry snowmelt from the polar regions of Mars to thirsty gardens in the temperate regions of the planet. He tracked the waxing and waning of the polar caps with the changing Martian seasons, and he was certain that he could also see a synchronized progression and recession of zones darkened by vegetation.

Lowell extrapolated. What he thought he was seeing, he was actually imagining. He was seeing something, but he connected dots that were really there in ways that weren't really there. Percival Lowell made drawings—beautiful drawings—and he had persuasive logic built upon what he thought he saw. It stirred the imagination. Perhaps, in the end, his kick to humanity's imagination was more important than being wrong about the details. He connected us to another world. In doing that, he changed the one around him.

Later, the fine observatory that Lowell established became the workshop for several professional astronomers of historical note, among them being young Clyde Tombaugh. Less famous, but probably not less significant, was V.M. Slipher who, in the 1920s, collected the first evidence that virtually all other galaxies are rushing away from our own Milky Way. Slipher's work provided the impetus for Edwin Hubble's startling discovery, announced in 1929, that the whole of the universe is rapidly expanding. And then we knew—nothing ever stays the same. Hubble himself connected a lot of flimsy dots. His extrapolations were probably just as flimsy as the ones Lowell made, but Hubble was lucky enough to have guessed correctly.

Prior to Hubble's discovery, scientists thought the universe was essentially static. Albert Einstein even inserted an extra term into his equations for gravity trying to force them to describe a static universe, never questioning the assumption despite the fact that his brilliant theory really demanded a universe on the go. The expansion of the universe was one of three discoveries between the mid 1920's and the mid 1960's that changed humankind's place in the scheme of things. First, the enormous scale of the universe started to become apparent. Then, the uniform expansion of the universe was revealed. Finally, the fading light of the fiery beginning of the universe was observed. We live in the dissipating glow of the super nuclear flash that spawned space and time and all that now exists within them.

With the discovery of the primordial fireball, cherished notions about the nature of existence that civilizations had cultivated, recorded, and believed for millennia were vaporized. We are the first generation to know the broad epochs in the history of the universe, and we are still adjusting to this knowledge. There *is* a meaning to what lies beyond the horizon. But what is it? Reality is distilled from the reality that surrounds it. Remoteness exists mostly in imagination.

The processes of existence can be counter-intuitive. The expansion of the universe created the near vacuum that Nature filled in with stars, planets and living beings. Somewhat ironically, the expansion of the universe postpones Helmholtz's heat death by continuously lowering the temperature at which the ultimate equilibrium will occur. The process has a limit—called the temperature of absolute zero. When heat death does finally overtake the cosmos, the expansion of the universe will make it more like freezing to death. The real death of the universe will come from the slowing and stretching and severing of all the connections in the quilt of existence.

As I ride, always in the back of my mind is the knowledge that *all* events have a beginning and an end—and that sometimes empty places get filled in with things that cannot be predicted.

When the door to the observatory is opened, I see that the great telescope fills the width of the "dome." I recall seeing encyclopedia photos of both the structure and the telescope when I was a boy, dreaming about big telescopes of my own. It was bigger in my dreams.

I can see the directness and simplicity of each part of the scope: knobs attached to shafts, linking to gears that turn a saddle or beam—plates riveted to plates, bolted to a disc or a ring to hold some optic in place. I could have imagined these mechanisms when I was twelve—could have built them in those same dreams.

The old scope in its odd wooden dome is more sculpture than instrument—a monument to the hope that just one imagination still matters in a world that no longer seems to care about just one of anything. Percival Lowell is buried close to his telescope, but some of his extrapolations still scatter seed.

After my visit to the observatory, I descended swiftly from Mars Hills, finding the main corridor into town that had eluded me on the way up. It had been a fun visit. I turned south on Arizona Route 89A and negotiated the traffic and the signal lights around the Northern Arizona University campus. I was intent on cruising out of town.

Then I spotted a Schlotzsky's Deli in a strip mall on the right hand side of the road. I braked hard and leaned right. Schlotzsky's is a homegrown piece of Austin and reminded me of home, or at least what used to be home. At any rate, it was my favorite deli sandwich. I'd worry about the semantics later. What a surprise! I wasn't hungry, but I wasn't going to let that little problem get in my way. I ordered a large one! Besides, I was easily burning 5,000 or more calories per day. Hey, what did they have for dessert? I always needed fuel.

It was a fun stop. But now I had to concentrate as I pedaled south on Route 89A. Many motorhomes chugged along the highway, and although I was sure the folks driving them were well-meaning and good-natured, some of them just didn't have a good grasp for how much of the road they were using.

Pine trees thickly lined the route, and there wasn't much of a vista. But the monotony tore suddenly at the top of the deep switchbacks that descend steeply into Oak Creek Canyon. The brink exposed the distances into the canyon below and across much of the area to the south and east. Higher terrain restricted the panorama a bit more to the west and cut it off back to the north. I was surprised that none of this area was very desert-like, and whatever color the rocks might be, they are mostly hidden beneath a thick mantle of green. However, I doubted my route will be blessed with so much shade from beginning to end.

With some swishing of air and clicking of the freewheel, I weaved down the switchbacks and into the canyon. It was fun! I followed the

creek on the downhill grade for a ways, and then found a small campground without many tourists called Pine Flat and made a home for
the night. Shade and the gurgling of the creek greeted me. But these
pleasantries competed with traffic noise and stinky exhaust from the
well-used highway, punctuated by the screeching of people having noisy
fun along the creek. It was not quite paradise, but at least it had a
couple of the ingredients.

Total mileage for the day: 41.1 Total mileage for the trip: 1597.9

## Day 39:

I trickled out of Oak Creek Canyon in little sporadic spurts, like a
window shopper moving through a market, stopping frequently to
admire but not long enough to buy. Despite my sputtering start, I rolled
into Sedona before most of the tourists had finished breakfast. I made
a call to Eileen. She and Nancy were still tied to the calendar that I
mostly ignored. The earliest the two of them could meet me at Grand
Canyon was just over two weeks away. I still had some time to kill.

*Oak Creek Canyon*

Traffic in Sedona was heavy, fast and preoccupied—with a lot of big motorhomes stirred into the mix. Exploring the city on bicycle didn't seem very safe to me. From the bits of Sedona that I could see, it lacked the charm of Durango, Silverton and Flagstaff. It didn't seem like a bad little town, but it projected a more commercial and less historical face than the other three. I prospected for a quart of cold orange juice and then pumped out of town on 89A towards Cottonwood.

The famous red rock scenery around Sedona is certainly worthy of its reputation. When I think of Sedona, the first things that come to mind are western movies and John Wayne. I was more moved by John Wayne's recent death than I would have guessed. I had seen many of his movies, yet didn't consider myself a particularly avid fan of his. But he had been a constant of sorts. He was just always there. And no matter how flawed the character he played, I knew that in the end he would find a way to do a noble thing.

Constants are hard to find, hard to trust, and hard to forget once you do trust them. I am frequently amazed that a person can wake up still being the same person that she or he was before going to bed— that memory, personality and cognitive ability have so much continuity.

It's hard enough to accept that electrical forces can hold the substance and shape of our bodies intact so well. That the physical functioning of those same bodies is so consistent is even more remarkable, drawing upon a hidden scheme that includes a dash of magic. While individual functions can be plausibly linked to the physical gears and ratchets of the body, how does it all get coordinated into an overall scheme that is identifiably human—and stay consistent from day to day?

The bits and pieces that coordinate to form the mind are even less tangible than those of the body. They are almost supernatural, extending beyond the physical elements of the brain alone. What critical mass of ethereal elements is needed to hold a consciousness together like gravity holds the sun together?

Maybe people aren't so constant after all. Perhaps consciousness fluctuates with quantum-like randomness. Maybe we just aren't equipped to notice the fluctuations and float in an illusion of continuity. Believing in a person is believing in a mystery. The chemicals and the structures can account for most of what we are—but not quite all. Beyond forces, there must be scheme.

Moving towards Cottonwood, the terrain becomes broader and less verdant. I am descending into a wide desert-like valley. As I pedal into Cottonwood, I am reminded of Farmington, a working place without time or reason for imagination. The cottonwood is one of my favorite trees, providing good shade along dry streambeds where other trees would wilt and die. I guess I expected some kind of solitary oasis here, but the buzz of commerce is what I have found, instead.

It's very hot already, so I stop at a convenience store for a cold drink and snack. I'm sure that there will be no Schlotzsky's here. I turn south on Arizona Route 279 and head towards Camp Verde, about fifteen miles further down the uninspiring highway. At least the road has a bit of downhill slope.

The map on top of my handlebar bag indicates that I am cycling through the Prescott National Forest, but I can't see a tree anywhere. Two canteens later, I reach the interstate and cross under. Two and a half miles later, I wheel into the burg of Camp Verde, which doesn't appear to be much more than a few uninviting buildings arranged in a little grid, and some dogs wandering listlessly in the afternoon heat, too tired to even chase or bark at me. There is a small state historical site marking the old frontier fort that once provided refuge here. But it doesn't provide refuge today since there is no camping at the site. I don't think I would have been inclined to stay, anyway. Then I pass a forest service ranger station and I'm thinking, "Yeah, right. What forest?" It's still early, and I've got time to ride for a few more hours, but it's looking like tonight's campsite might be cobbled more from necessity than good opportunity.

About six miles beyond Camp Verde, I approach a thick line of large trees: magnificent trees, actually. There is a sign reading Clear Creek Campground. This wasn't on my map! And sure enough, there is also a lively running clear creek—plus nice, shaded tables, and potable water from a hand pump. There is absolutely no one else here, and I haven't seen a single vehicle since I left Camp Verde. I can take a canteen shower!

It wasn't located where I thought it would be, but maybe I have found a little paradise, after all. I decide to stay.

Total mileage for the day: 54.0

## Day 40—Mile 1651:

I stayed up through much of last night watching the waning moon make its way across the almost still desert. The valley around me was a calico of silver and gray. The cottonwoods tiptoed around their shadows like synchronized sleepwalkers.

A desert night is not the closed and claustrophobic thing that a forest night can be. A desert night is a gentle waltzing partner for a restless mind. A desert night stirs the embers of memory—plays pantomime with an almost forgotten lover.

The sounds of the desert night are unhurried, almost slow motion—like a dream. They draw semiconscious effort, a resistant bending of the awareness, rather than an unsettling start.

But the desert night is too expansive to be friendly—too primordial to be familiar. It picks at the recesses of your spirit that you thought were so well hidden.

The moon hanging long before the desert horizon conjured an endless highway with but a single passenger. Its muted light fell through the tree branches and settled between the scattered stones like the sad recollections of a lost hope—now searching for a new reality.

I was uncertain why, but I decided to make a layover at Clear Creek for one more night. In the afternoon, two motorhomes entered the campground together. They were occupied by two retired couples that were not shy about introducing themselves. They inquired about my travels and listened with genuine curiosity and even seemed a bit impressed. They invited me to join their group later, and I hung out with them until well after dark. The conversation shifted away from

me, and I learned about their nomadic lifestyle that covered the calendar: gypsies from Cleveland on extended tour. They were staying at the Clear Creek Campground for a couple of nights until they could get into a private campground with facilities back in Camp Verde for a much longer stay. They would even be able to get mail there. It would be their home for a while.

The night grew much cooler than the previous one had been. The two women went inside to escape the chill. The men stood around looking at the stars, then adjourned as the yellow glow in the east signaled that the moon would soon rise.

I was still awake when she peeked through the screen door of my tent.

## Day 41:

I packed all my cogitations into my panniers and let myself loose on a fantastic morning ride!

It was all uphill, but it was great: a steady grade without the annoying little dips that reverse one's progress. I vaulted from desert to forest, onto a high mesa about 4,000 feet above the 3,100-foot elevation of the Clear Creek Campground. The morning started clear and refreshingly cool, and I climbed just quickly enough to stay ahead of the heating desert air. The view was so good that I didn't mind the pull at all. I just took my time—even did a little singing to myself and enjoyed the vista.

The area this side of Clear Creek reminded me of Big Bend National Park in Texas, where I have spent so much time. In the low elevations, I started the morning surrounded by creosote, juniper, and piñon. On slopes that were a little higher, agave (or century plant) was added to the mix.

As I gained elevation, the view widened. Looking back to the western bank of the long, deep desert valley, I saw banded cliffs of red and cream, brightly lit as they faced the morning sun. Casner and Black Mountains waved from beyond the cliff line, thirty-five miles to the northwest. Continuous veins of shiny green trees lined the waterways and split the valley into tapered shards. I could just make out the thread of gray over which I had ridden and could see where it crossed the heavy green vein of Clear Creek, the campground hidden somewhere within it. The moon, nearing the last-quarter phase, hung above the cliffs, easily seen against the very dark blue sky.

Nearing the top of the grade and entering the vegetation zone dominated by Ponderosa Pines, the vista opened in other directions. North Peak was visible twenty-five miles to the south, in the Mazatzal Wilderness, and Humphrey's Peak was clearly visible fifty-five miles to the north, between the Grand Canyon and me. For the second time, my line of sight connected me to Humphrey's Peak, from different perspectives and distances.

In the span of a few hours, I rode *Intrepid* from one world into another world that was distinctly different. And for the moment, I was able to create a visual connection from one world to the other, measuring its length by the joy and effort of my ride. I told myself I would like to do more riding in this region sometime in the future—maybe with someone, also in my future. Then I pedaled down the road, away from the edge.

The day clouded up, but I didn't mind. My shadow needed the rest. Besides, the clouds kept the day cool. The gray light dulled the green walls of dense forest that crowded both sides of the road. This day will be much cooler, indeed—the coolness being constantly replenished by a slight northerly breeze. The feeling of summer had fled, at least for the morning.

Suddenly, a large, furry coyote, the furriest I have ever seen, ran out of the forest to my left, chasing a rabbit. The coyote didn't appear to see me at first, and I judged that we were on a near-collision course. The rabbit, obviously in high gear, scooted past the front wheel of *Intrepid* about the same time the coyote finally saw me. I don't think an animal could reverse directions more quickly than the coyote did. It was if it had bounced off a wall. It ran back into the forest without ever looking back or slowing down. I also encountered a baby rattlesnake that would not slither off the road despite my *careful* urgings.

I stopped for the night at Clint's Well Campground. The inviting name to the contrary, the campground had no running water. Fortunately, I carried a good supply.

Mileage for the day: 41.9

## Day 42:

I cycled north from Clint's Well Campground along a paved but skinny forest service road. I passed through Happy Jack, not really large enough to call a town or even a village. Only one or two cars passed me during the first twenty-five miles of my ride.

The first really striking thing I came to was the initial view of Mormon Lake. From a distance, the lake looked large and deep. When I got closer, I saw it was more marsh than lake and was rich with waterfowl: floating, standing on stilt-like legs in the middle of the water, or scooting and bobbing on shorter stick-like legs around the edges of the water. The sound of all those birds was like a symphony, not in full concert, but warming up before the concert. All around, there were squeaks and squeals, honks and hoots, and trills and trumpets—all stacked and compressed against one another.

As I neared the lake, I reached a fork in the road. Straight ahead would be the shortest route back to Flagstaff, but I bent left to circle the fascinating marsh, masquerading as a lake. I stopped at a campground overlooking the lake to sit on a table for a while, make a sandwich, and absorb the noisy spectacle.

When I leaned *Intrepid* against a table, I discovered that I had lost my fuzzy long-sleeve Woolrich shirt. I always donned this favorite shirt as the first additional layer against a chill. In the early morning, I started my ride wearing the dark blue shirt. When the heat of the ride and the day began to build, I tucked the shirt under a strap, strung over my sleeping bag and tent, on the back rack. Usually, I fold and roll the shirt and put it back into a pannier. But this time, I took a lazy shortcut. And it cost me. The shirt had slipped from the strap somewhere along the ride. It was gone. I was upset.

I still had the lightweight jacket Eileen brought to me at Chaco, and I had my thin, nylon rain parka. But one important layer against the cold, the most comfortable and versatile layer and my favorite, was now gone. Damn!

I tried to shake the disappointment and return to the moment. I sat upon the table top in my usual pose, studying the area. Mormon Lake was really quite remarkable. Could I focus on that? And there were many people on bicycles around the lake. From where did they come? In addition to a couple of campgrounds, there were buildings that looked like resorts: motels and cottages. Maybe one or more of these businesses rented bicycles. None of the bikes were equipped with bags, and the riders clearly had not come very far.

After finishing my lunch, I continued on towards Flagstaff. I thought I might camp near Upper Lake Mary. But when I got to the campground, I discovered it was close to the highway, had no water, and wasn't very interesting. Three strikes! It was out! Maybe I was spoiled by the campground at Clear Creek. At any rate, there was still a lot of day left. So, I just pushed onward.

I had been so fussy that I didn't end up in a campground at all. Instead, I camped in the forest, about fifty yards from the road just outside Flagstaff, not far from the airport.

Total mileage for the day: 50.5

## Day 43:

I picked my way into Flagstaff, avoiding busy streets as much as I could. I spent the rest of the morning shopping, finding some of the items I needed. What I couldn't find, I would do without. About

noon, I treated myself to a vanilla malt and headed out of town
along US Route 180, going north and west towards the Grand
Canyon.

The day was beautiful and bright, but with a few high cirrus
clouds and a strong north wind that faced me. Autumn was blowing
southward. The coolness of the air lapped against the warmth
generated on the skin by the rays of sunlight that still pointed with
a summer-like aim. The confluence created a confusing mix of
sensations but also a pleasing mix, like chocolate swirled with
vanilla.

I was flirting with Humphrey's Peak again, making my third
connection to the 12,633-foot mountain that stands taller than
any other in Arizona. This time, I was much closer as I cast my
sightline. I saw the brilliant, seasonal patches of yellow and gold
quilting the green slopes of the great mountain. Earlier in the trip,
when I first spotted Humphrey's, it was from the opposite side of
the mountain. I was still on the Navajo Reservation, and
Humphrey's was just a blurry, blue bump on the horizon. Now, it
radiated with autumn colors and dominated the landscape. I was
connected from here to the mountain and from the mountain to
the bridge over the Little Colorado. I stopped for lunch in the shade
of a tree and savored a sandwich, the view of the mountain, and the
recollections of my earlier sightings of it. I felt a certain peace
because I knew where I was going next, but I could still see from
where I had been.

As I cranked my way up Route 180 that afternoon, I watched
Humphrey turn its head and shrink in the distance. Seeing a great
object up close is revealing. But sighting it from afar where others
might overlook it or not be able to appreciate its magnificence, is

magic. A connection across time and distance is the magic of the mind—whether the object is a mountain two days of riding away, or a galaxy faintly revealed by the focus of a backyard telescope.

At sunset, I docked at the Ten-X Campground in the Kaibab National Forest, just outside the national park. The canyon will have to wait one more night.

Total mileage for the day: 83.1 Total mileage for the trip: 1826.5

# 13. Grand Canyon Gravitation

From Humphrey's shadow, it's a long ride north across a broad rolling desert to reach the gently tilted forest. The distant desert view becomes lost to the jam of Ponderosa behind Ponderosa. Suddenly, the curtain ahead is torn and there is sky behind Ponderosa.

Almost without warning the horizon is bent, broken, and stood on end. Vision plunges ledge over ledge until your knees wobble and your step becomes tentative. The banded panorama beyond doesn't look real. There is a sudden silence to the world. All motion is wound backwards a few steps from the edge. At the base of this tortured, abrupt chasm—at the bottom of the world—snakes a sinuous crack that plummets in freefall to purgatory. At only a few scattered points across the vast, primordial landscape can one peer deep enough into the inner trench to see that hell is a cataract on the hungry Colorado.

No forest bandages the wound before you. The tear has not yet become a scar. The hard ridges and the vulnerable washes show the details of how the earth was gouged away, particle by tiny particle. Dismantled, hauled down into the abyss and carried away by a mercurial conveyor heeding the tireless call of gravity—the emptiness has left two billion years stranded along its banks.

Seas and deserts have come and gone. Dinosaurs were buried and turned to stone. The sky, once dark and murky, turned blue. Molecules rained from the sky and collected in the ooze—the ooze stirred and spilled life upon the mud flats—and humans stepped from the mud to hammer and chisel with stone, bringing voice and structure that had never existed through the eons. Even stars winked and died, and galaxies twirled around hundreds of times. A few inches of its depth dwarfs the longest lifetime.

Scale—in distance and in time. A mile deep. Two billion years.

## Day 44:

The night at Ten-X dived into a frigid calm at the 7,000-foot elevation, but I was okay in my sleeping bag. Early the next morning, the forest remained cold as I bicycled into the park. I grumbled at myself again for losing my comfortable, long-sleeved shirt along the road. However, when I neared the rim, a swirl of much warmer air rising out of the canyon greeted me.

I finally arrived at the place I had been zigzagging and circling towards ever since I left Canyonlands. My original plan would have taken me south from Monticello, through Mexican Hat to Monument Valley and Kayenta, and then turned me directly towards the Grand Canyon after crossing the Little Colorado. Six weeks into it, my journey had already spanned twice the time and distance I originally intended—and I was still going.

I biked over to the sprawling Mather Campground to secure a site. This camping area, along with the lodges and stores and dining halls, approaches the mass of a small city. I was happy to learn the campground included a walk-in area perfect for my needs and only costing fifty cents per night. I set up my campsite and went to check out another amenity of this city lifestyle: a hot shower. The showers operated by coin, and I took enough coins for two cycles.

After taking a shower, I encountered a couple in the campground that had been traveling by bicycle with their four-year old son for 112 days, covering 5,800 miles to this point. The husband towed their son in a trailer behind his bike. I found it interesting that they abandoned the normal calendar, counting days from the start of their trip, instead—just as I did.

The sheer magnitude of their accomplishments could have easily deflated me, but I reminded myself that I had done things I never imagined I could do. My trip was about *discovering*, not about *proving*.

However, the encounter seemed to plant an indistinct seed in my head about future explorations having dimensions that I could only vaguely imagine now. I wasn't deflated, but I felt incomplete.

With most of my gear tucked into my tent, I pedaled along West Rim Drive with a noticeably lightened load, at least on my bike. Perhaps this is the way it will be when I reach Santa Barbara. I will be traveling with a noticeably lighter load—but slightly heavier heart.

## Day 45:

At sunrise, I broke camp and bicycled to Grandview Point. I was embarking on an overnight hike into the canyon, even though I didn't have backpacking gear with me. My only pack was a small lightweight knapsack for day hiking. I would need to improvise.

The plan was to hide *Intrepid* and remaining gear in the forest within a mile of the trailhead. I found a good spot and then started assembling my load for the hike. I reluctantly decided to leave my tent behind. Chances of a storm were remote, but I preferred to keep the biting things at bay. The tiny pack enforced some choices, however. I tied my sleeping bag to the bottom of the pack and stuffed everything else inside except for one canteen in its insulated cover. I tied this to a belt loop on my shorts.

Okay, it was a bit makeshift, but I carried what I needed, strapped to my body in one way or another. I laid *Intrepid* on its side and walked out of the forest, carefully memorizing the route back to my bike. I hoped that I could find it again! I walked the road to the trailhead and then descended three miles into the canyon along the Grandview Trail to Horseshoe Mesa, so named for its curving U-shape. Horseshoe Mesa floats in a middle zone of the canyon, suspended about halfway between the top and bottom, a little closer to the top.

I camped alone on the mesa. The South Rim hid the sunset. The top of the canyon wall below the North Rim turned red, then pink. The sky faded from steel blue, to gray, and then to black. The canyon slowly evaporated into darkness. There were no events, just steady transitions. It was dead calm and dead silent. I was lonely.

I didn't sleep well. I was constantly on alert, waiting for some crawly thing to invade my sleeping bag. It never happened. Except for a few flies and a raven, I neither saw nor heard any animals. I spent much time looking at the star-filled sky. I saw one meteor that was so bright it momentarily lit up the ground. It stained a patch of sky with a visible trail that took several seconds to dissipate.

When the wind settled just before sunset, the canyon began filling with smoke from a controlled burn on the North Rim, set by the Forest Service. Within a few hours, the smoke in the canyon was thick enough that my breathing was somewhat uncomfortable. A few hours before dawn, an easterly breeze cleared the canyon a bit. I slept from exhaustion.

## Day 46:

I collected my things and went to explore the mesa before heading back up to the South Rim. Prior to starting the hike, I purchased a skinny guidebook about the trails in the canyon. This guidebook mentioned a cave located near some mining ruins on the mesa. I calculated that the cave and ruins were off to the east of me, so I went in that direction. I found the ruins and then the cave. The cave looked interesting, but the dense blackness and silence down the cave's ragged throat conjured an image of being swallowed whole. I was spared agonizing over whether to continue: the batteries in my stubby yellow flashlight didn't have much juice left in them. So, I wasn't able to go very far into the cave, never leaving the zone wetted by a little seeping daylight.

While looking around the mesa, I encountered a very obnoxious couple with a dog. Having a dog in the canyon is a definite no-no according to the park regulations. Then I came to an old miner's shack that had been vandalized, and I observed dog food inside the shack. Okay, I did a little adding of the clues and decided that I knew who had done what. I hiked out of the canyon with a little extra zip in my step, making it a mission to let the rangers know what I had seen as quickly as I could.

I located *Intrepid* without any trouble, and all was as I left it. I scurried to the ranger station at Desert View to return my hiking permit and report the mischief on the mesa. Heavy traffic along the road, including a multitude of motorhomes, created an air of tension and exhaust fumes. One motorhome in particular came dangerously close to me, missing me by only a few inches even though there was no oncoming traffic and plenty of room to swing out around me.

Heading back to Mather from Desert View, I stopped at most of the canyon overlooks. At one overlook, my faith was boosted when I met a couple in another motorhome. They handed me raisins and took a photo of me.

Nearing Mather, the bracket supporting my handlebar bag suddenly snapped: a significant problem. Without this bag, there wasn't sufficient space to carry my gear, and the load on my bicycle would not be properly distributed front-to-rear.

I reclaimed my spot in the walk-in campground, erected my little home, and headed for the showers. I decided to settle into city life for a few days, Grand Canyon style.

Later, I browsed through the store trying to figure out some way to repair the broken bracket or to improvise a replacement. I quickly realized that I faced a very cantankerous situation. I was depressed and doped myself with some ice cream.

When I returned to my campsite, I encountered a fellow from England who had been hitchhiking in the United States for three months. He related that there was someone camped nearby who might be able to solve my problem. He would try to introduce me to him soon.

The village contained several dining rooms and food concessions. Near dark, I ambled back to the one next to the supermarket and took a break from my routine of building sandwiches. I noticed several other folks from the walk-in campground foraging for dinner at the same establishment.

When I finished my dinner and went back outside, there was another bike leaned against the windows close to mine: a beautiful new bike of black, green and gold. It was the fanciest bike I had ever seen. It sported best-you-can-get Campagnolo brakes and gears and shifters and so forth—along with best-of-everything-else leather saddle, handlebars and accessories. It included a triple crank and eighteen gears. And it was equipped for touring with matching green, best-you-can-get Kirtland bags, the whole set including front panniers.

This shiny new bicycle cost more to custom build than my bike, camping gear, camera gear and entire trip cost, together. My bike was good, but it seemed shabby parked next to this gem. While I unlocked *Intrepid*, the owner of the black beauty came out and introduced himself. Don was his name. He explained that he was a Notre Dame fan and had the custom *King of Tour* Mercian frame on his bike painted accordingly.

He said he was at the canyon for a few days by himself, and he wondered if he could camp near me. So, off we went, the prince and the pauper.

## Day 47:

I squirmed out of my tent before sunrise and biked to an overlook. Don, too, was up and led the way. Smoke from the forest service burn on the North Rim filled the canyon, smudging and hiding details. But the smoke accentuated the many layers of distance created by the sequences of ridges, mesas, buttes and towers—sorting them by depth of shadow and shade of blue.

The deliberate sequencing of my gear, however, had been disturbed by the broken bracket for my front bag. Even bicycling around the rim was less convenient without the handlebar bag. Camera gear, canteen and map were now banished to a pannier on the back rack. I was anxious to fix the broken bracket.

After watching the sunrise and having breakfast along the rim, I told Don I would meet him later and went searching for the Grand Canyon post office. I had given Barbara the approximate date of my arrival and mentioned it might be possible for me to receive a letter addressed for general delivery. It was a subtle reference slipped into one of my letters. I wasn't expecting a reply. But when I asked at the window, the clerk stunned me by presenting a blue envelope. I opened the envelope as I stepped out of the post office. In addition to a letter, Barbara enclosed a small photo of herself. I was still shocked as I pedaled back to my campsite. Barbara had written to me!

I met Don and gathered some lunch from the diner next to the store. We sat at a picnic table in the cool, pine-scented air. While I ate my lunch, I couldn't resist reading Barbara's letter again. I started thinking about my reply, but I would not be able to convey to her the lift she had given me. Out of all the chaos I left in Austin, I had discovered a surprising hidden ember I knew would glow a very long time. I wished I had gotten to know her better—but it simply would not have been possible. Maybe the future would unveil a surprise.

As Don and I ate, a small succession of people asked to sit at our table and then struck up conversations. Some of these folks were recently acquainted with each other, but no one seemed to know everyone else. The more people that sat, the more connections beckoned for others to join. A little club of travelers was forming spontaneously at the table, like an embryonic star gathering gas from a surrounding nebula. The folks in this group seemed very different from one another, but all had gravitated to the Grand Canyon as if drawn by some force. All had come alone from some distance, and all were staying long enough to absorb something from being here.

The English hitchhiker joined the group, which had now spilled over to a second table. Not long afterward, another fellow joined us, and the Englishman said aloud, "Charles, this is the guy who might be able to help you."

The last fellow was a machinist by trade. Middle-aged, he had quit his job and decided to travel after a divorce left him depressed and purposeless. He was on the road to find himself again. The draw of the Grand Canyon had pulled him here and held him awhile. He didn't know how long his search would take. So, he outfitted a ten foot travel trailer with a bed and a miniature shop. He took on repairs, mostly to motorhomes and trailers, to support his gypsy lifestyle. It wasn't a permanent arrangement, but it would substitute for a life until he found his again.

For three dollars, he would weld the pieces of my broken bracket. He was willing to fix it for less, if three dollars was a problem for me. I whipped out the three dollars and handed it to him asking, "Are you sure this is enough?" He spared me from deep trouble, and three dollars seemed cheap.

That evening, the little group bound by Grand Canyon gravity gathered spontaneously, once more. This group cradled some sadness but also held a measure of hope and joy. The gravity of the canyon tugged at the heavy core of this little star made of gypsies, but it brought a few things to the surface, as well.

## Day 48:

Don's itinerary did not include touring by bicycle on this trip. Starting by car from his home in New Jersey, a buddy of his dropped him at the Grand Canyon and continued on to California with the car. When his buddy returned, the two of them would go to Big Bend National Park in Texas for some rafting on the Rio Grande. So, for now, Don was hanging out and having fun riding his fancy new bicycle around the South Rim.

Don and I launched from the village at sunrise, headed for a hike in the canyon along the Kaibab trail. The trail started at Yaki Point, a couple of miles from the campground, so we needed to ride our bikes to the trailhead. By the time we hid our bikes in the forest and started down the trail, it was approaching 8:30. Don wore a watch, and I was immediately reminded of the attention that a clock demands.

We were both in good condition and sped down the trail without really trying. Don was several years younger than I and a bit of an anomaly in the wayfarers club. The others all were mending some kind of wound or looking for some kind of answer. Don was just looking for fun. Back home, he had a girlfriend, a job, and a life that was okay for him. Taking trips and having adventures was part of that life.

I asked about his fancy Mercian bicycle. Without needing to think about his answer, he responded that most of life is a compromise beyond his control. He decided to do this one thing that mattered to him and was within his control without any compromises.

We almost hiked to the Colorado, stopping just short at a good overlook of the suspension bridges. We ate our lunches much more slowly than we had walked, and then we headed back up the trail in a flurry and some dust. We rescued our bikes from the forest at 1:45, so Don's watch said. I was not tired and could have easily done double the distance at the same cadence.

I sat alone between meetings at the Wayfarers' picnic table and finished writing the letter to Barbara I had started the afternoon before. In it I wrote, "Of all the wonders I have seen and experienced, the greatest wonder is to think about a person far beyond my horizon and know that she thought about me today."

### Days 49 to 51:

These days blurred one into another. I fell into a routine of village life: bicycling along the rim with Don; going to overlook points for sunrises and sunsets; eating hot meals with the Wayfarers Club; sitting on the bench rather than on the table top; taking hot showers that were two cycles long; wiggling into my tent at night and staring up at the starry skies with just a bit of longing and a little water around the eyes. I wondered in awe how a couple could spin a bond so marvelous that they wove an epic bicycle journey for three spanning almost 6,000 miles. In contrast, I sifted through the lonely ashes of accidental wayfarers—and I thought of Barbara from the sadness of an impossible dream.

## Days 52 and 53:

Don left the Grand Canyon the previous afternoon with his buddy who had the car. The Wayfarers Club started to dissolve. Several others departed as well.

I was still waiting for Eileen and Nancy and had time to explore. I decided not to waste it and got a permit for an overnight hike to Tanner Rapids. The park ranger in the backcountry office didn't like to issue permits to solo hikers, especially for the primitive trails. So, I had to do a little persuading to get the permit in hand.

I followed the same general plan as before, hiding *Intrepid* in the forest, and stuffing and tying things to my little daypack until I looked like a refugee from a flea market. This time I tied my tent to the pack, as well. I was sure that the ranger who issued me the solo permit would regret her decision if she saw my makeshift rigging.

Appearances aside, the hike went well. It was a great trail and a great campsite. The nearby Palisades of the Desert epitomized my vision of a Grand Canyon wall. Near the bottom of the canyon, I saw a sidewinder suddenly churn its way to the surface, out of bare sand, one step ahead of my stride. The motion of the rattlesnake was so oddly mesmerizing. The corkscrewing snake changed my perspective. I didn't take any other sandbar for granted. Bare might not be bare, after all.

## Day 54:

By the time I returned to the campground, the last members of The Wayfarers Club were gone. I fell back into solitary remnants of my village routine. Some of the empty spaces that had been temporarily filled echoed once more.

Near sunset, I biked along the West Rim Drive to Pima Point. I leaned my bicycle against the rock wall that guarded the overlook and kept tourists from falling over the edge. I hopped up onto the wall for a better look at the canyon that was already beginning to glow orange with the last filtering of the day. Yes, I was back to sitting on table tops. Ah, how easily civilized ways can slip from the desert rat when he returns to his natural habitat!

Pima was the point farthest from the lodges, towards the end of the drive. People were assembling, but the congregation was not large. A film crew, French I judged from the words that were said, had set up to capture the view.

As I was surveying the canyon, the director of the French film crew turned towards me and looked straight into my eyes. He never gestured, and we didn't speak—but I could tell what he wanted me to do. He signaled his crew discreetly. The camera swung over, and then I began: I folded my arms and faced the canyon from the top of the wall, my blue bike at my feet. Slowly and deliberately, I panned my head from one end of the vista to the other, and then back again. When I was done, the director nodded and gave a faint smile, more with his eyes than his mouth. I had given what he wanted—perhaps more than he expected in the dusk at the overlook.

## Day 55:

I hiked the Kaibab Trail, once again—this time going all the way to the first bridge. I scorched the route: down and back up in a flash.

## Day 56:

I phoned Eileen for a final check. She and Nancy would be on their way the next day. Since arriving at the canyon, I have bicycled a total of 139.5 miles along the South Rim.

**Day 57:**

Eileen and Nancy arrived from Austin. They flew into Las Vegas and then rented a car. We secured a campsite in the regular Mather Campground and set out to explore the rim from their car. We watched thunderstorms veil and splash the canyon from Yavapai Point until we could feel static in our hair. We first retreated to the cover of the museum and then settled into dinner at Thunderbird Lodge. It was good to have company again.

**Day 58:**

Eileen, Nancy and I hiked down the Bright Angel Trail to the oasis at Indian Gardens, then on along Garden Creek to the overlook at the top of the inner gorge. Eileen and Nancy were adjusting to the rigors of the trail, and we spent most of the afternoon on the climb back to the rim. Spirits were high all the way up, and no blisters were rubbed. Dinner at the Thunderbird tasted especially good.

**Day 59:**

The band of three headed out early on the main hike that we had planned, an overnight backpacking excursion down the primitive Hermit Trail and camping at the river.

Nancy had a bit of a balance problem because of a condition with her ear, so we fashioned a hiking stick for her from the tall, dried stalk of an agave plant, now bloomed and dead. It was just what she needed.

At one point along the trail—in a huge slab of rock, broken away and tilted almost vertical—we encountered the tracks of a small reptile or amphibian that were left some 300 million years ago, now frozen in the Coconino Sandstone. I tried to reach across the eons—imagining the creature on its day in the sun, moving in little bursts and then pausing for the next impulse to arrive.

The ancient animal touched the earth that day to leave an imprint on this day, but it was not this rock that it touched. Perhaps it meandered across a sandy mudflat that seemed cool and inviting leaving tracks that later hardened and were buried and processed into stone by the forces and events of the earth. The creature did not amble in the Grand Canyon because the canyon did not yet exist. It is not only a different time that I tried to imagine but also a different world.

Deep in the Grand Canyon, a vast cross-section of time and space engulfed me; the entire sweep of it was blurring and disorienting. Lodged within this mighty array, the fossilized tracks of the creature long gone provided a startling point of focus: a sudden and unexpected connection to a single moment in time at a single place by a single living creature. In this deep graveyard of time, the creature flickered in and out of existence in a brief blink and then was buried by the uncountable sequence of blinks stacked up the canyon walls. Amongst the tangle and the blur, a connection jumped out that was one-to-one, instant-to-instant, and creature-to-creature—across the eons. The sensation was powerful.

I realized that all through my trip I have been trying to weave myself into a larger tapestry, perhaps seeking some meaning in the face of being so small and temporary against a universe that is so large and lasting. I am a mere flicker in the midst of my day in the sunlight. But I have part of my answer—maybe all the answer that can be. Life is what you make it while you still have the time.

## Day 60:

Rain rattled the tent shell that night, and the morning never radiated in its usual way. When I exited my tent and surveyed the curious gray sky, I saw something that I had a hard time believing. The upper third of the canyon was draped with curtains of snow. Close to the rim, the canyon walls were essentially blanketed with snow, except on the vertical faces.

Well, none of the three of us prepared for this. I only had my shorts, light shirt, and nylon rain parka. Worse, I wore almost smooth-bottomed shoes intended mostly for cycling. Eileen and Nancy had only slightly more warm clothing than I did, but at least they wore hiking shoes. Nancy, however, had the balance problem that would be a liability on sloped, icy surfaces. It wasn't a good situation, but it was the one that we had.

The freezing cold did not sink to the bottom of the canyon, although it was cool and occasionally wet. We packed our stuff and prepared for an uncertain trudge to the top.

We began encountering some ice and snow about half way up. Mostly, we were just cold. We kept moving to stay warm. We barely paused for anything, although we were not hiking fast, just steadily. Clearly, we would not rest until we reached the top, assuming we could.

I anticipated one stretch of trail from the trip down. It worried me a lot. It was a steep set of switchbacks along a sheer drop in a sandstone wall. When we got there, it looked as dreadful as I had imagined it would. The trail was covered in a sheet of ice by what must have been a waterfall, now frozen. It cascaded from level to level, down the set of switchbacks—punctuated by long icicles grinning like walruses.

I had been following Eileen and Nancy up the trail. When we got to this area, they just stopped, and we all stared silently for a few moments. One of us finally said, "This looks really bad," but I'm not sure who said it because we were all thinking it.

I took the lead, but I didn't know what to expect or do. Some stones with their jagged tops barely poked up through the ice. I suggested, "Let's try to step on those." It was a terrible gamble and a heart-pounding, short-breathing five minutes, but we made it through the switchbacks. We knew we had been lucky.

The rest of the way proved cold and unpleasant, but after surviving the test of the icefall, no one complained. Eileen and Nancy remained cheerful and laughing despite being cold and tired. Eileen was a wisecracker by nature and kept us well stocked with one line jokes.

We crested the rim in mid-afternoon, although it took a clock, not the sun, to gauge the time. After warming ourselves by the huge fireplace in Bright Angel Lodge, we treated ourselves to a special meal in the dining room. It was snowing hard outside, and over a foot of the stuff had already piled on the ground. So we knew that we could not linger for too long. Eileen and Nancy would take the redeye flight home, but we probably needed to get out of the snow zone before dark since the roads would freeze.

We had stored *Intrepid*, with both wheels removed, in the backseat of their rental car while we hiked in the canyon. To make room for me to ride, I used Eileen's foam sleeping mat to cushion my bike and tied it to the top of the car. Darkness was dropping quickly by the time we passed the Seligman exit on I-40 and began to lose enough altitude to escape the snow.

At Kingman, Eileen turned right on US Route 93. A dense, black night enveloped the car. The urge to sleep stroked my consciousness seductively. I don't know how Eileen kept alert to drive. I nodded off a few times as I listened to the soft music of two female voices in the front seat. The plan was to drop me at a campground on the shore of Lake Mead. I remember waking to see the lights over the roadway and the blackness over the edge of Hoover Dam.

Within twenty minutes, I stood alone in the night, watching the taillights of the rental car disappear down the road. Then it hit me. I would not be going home.

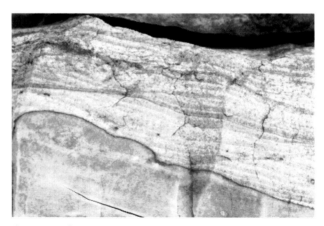

*An uncomformity—missing layers in the cross-section of time exposed in the Grand Canyon*

# 14. Sideways to Santa Barbara

## Day 61—Mile 1966:

No more friends from Austin will visit. The past is behind me—almost. One person lingers in my thoughts, but I doubt I will ever see her again. The discovery came too late and would have been too awkward if recognized earlier. I look at the little photo of Barbara that came in her general-delivery letter at Grand Canyon.

For the first time since I started this trip, I feel the urgent need to move on. I have tasks awaiting me at the end of this road. I have one more major waypoint before concluding my ride, but I am now riding with a sense of purpose towards what feels like my destination. My bags are packed, and *Intrepid* awaits me. I fold the final map to expose the last two legs of the ride on flipsides and tuck it into the map pocket of my handlebar bag—then slip the little photo into the corner of the map pocket window. Barbara will ride with me the remaining way to Santa Barbara. I power out of the campground towards Las Vegas. I am anxious and driven.

The campground at Boulder Beach is part of a larger complex that includes a marina and lodge. I lose track of days, but I'm guessing that it's not a weekend. It's quiet now. Boulder Beach would see a lot of action on a sunny weekend. I'm out of place here. It's not an unpleasant spot but more recreational than the stops to which I am accustomed.

I have covered so much territory and improvised so much of my route that is not practical for me to carry a detailed set of maps. I am a bit uncertain about picking my way through the area around Las Vegas. I decide to go through Henderson and take 146 over to Inter-state 15, then follow the frontage road (that I hope exists) until I can connect with highway 160 to continue westward. I suspect there is a back way from Boulder Beach to Henderson, but my map doesn't show it. Thus, I'm banished to the main highway (US 93) through Boulder City. My plan seems forced and fuzzy, but I will ride and see where it takes me.

The road starts out okay, but the shoulders narrow from time to time, creating stretches where riding is nerve-wracking. The shoulders disappear altogether as I enter Boulder City. I stop at a store for a drink and a snack, mostly to get away from the close traffic for a while. Fortunately, the highway divides and the shoulders broaden as I exit Boulder City. The traffic is fairly light towards Henderson, and I can relax some and let my mind wander a bit.

As I ride, I note a new trend in the roadside debris—women's panties. By the time I reach Henderson, I've passed at least a half-dozen pair discarded along the road. Thinking back along the course of my journey, I cannot recall seeing any panties along the road prior to this morning. What's the deal?

Okay, something is going on. I conclude there must be a dating ritual thriving in Las Vegas that hasn't caught on in Utah and the Four Corners—letting fly with an irretrievable signal.

Well, Las Vegas may loosen inhibitions, boiling away the crust hiding nature's simple truths. While some amorous encounters are *only* about the moment, the simple honesty of expressed desire is striking.

Direct connection without pretence seeds intimacy—need to need—polar opposites. The simplest and the scariest truths between a man and a woman are the spontaneous ones that don't need explaining but do need clear recognition. The courage required to unambiguously announce sexual intention is electrifyingly personal. A rendezvous in the dark along a deserted highway can generate overlap and spark—stitching ionic bonds.

I whittle through Henderson, chipping at the impeded miles. The day sizzles as I follow state highway 146 to the interstate. As I had hoped, a frontage road shadows the interstate, and I race downhill, chased by the clatter and growl of semis and impatient autos. While crossing over the interstate, I can see Las Vegas off to the north, smothered by a gray-brown cloud that fuzzes the outlines and subdues the colors. A flooded river of vehicles surges beneath me and disappears into the haze. The fast torrent is disorienting to watch from above.

I paddle out of the swift current of the interstate and head upstream along Nevada 160. The fury fades behind me. Only a seep of traffic wetted the good road surface on highway 160. But it is hot and sunny; the headwind blows dry, and the grade tugs against me. The climbing is hard work. Except for the intensity of the sun, I am not minding the job. Although I don't know anyone where I'm going and have no place to stay, I feel the urgency of being headed home. The discontinuity in these thoughts feels strange, but I am excited by it.

A few houses squat in scattered clusters here and there along the highway. Most assume styles forbidden in city neighborhoods. The renegade structures include A-frames, domes, and mountain cabins with high-pitched roofs, big windows and second-floor decks. Some of the houses have wind-driven electrical generators, all busy chopping up the mid-day west wind.

The ride out of Las Vegas is unexpectedly scenic. As I climb, I pass through the Red Rocks Canyon Conservation Area and into the Toiyabe National Forest. I find a subconscious rhythm for my climb and my thoughts wander again.

I am not carrying a watch on my travel, but I am thinking about the mystery of clocks. How is it that by merely shaping the geometry of a mechanism—creating cogs and spindles and ratchets and the like, all arrayed into some sequence—that the mechanism can dip into the invisible current of time and be carried so perfectly and predictably? Everywhere around us, form connects to function. If a certain form is created, then a certain function seems to flow out of it as if a specific spirit had been waiting to occupy it.

There is a similarity between the hidden flow of time and the hidden flow of life. A person starts as a chemical reaction that if incubated in a certain way, proceeds to a certain form. But something unseen and harder to measure catches hold of the new form as it takes shape and animates it—like a clock begins ticking. This something, like the flow of time, is part of a larger current with a definite pattern. The sum is greater than the visible parts.

Two different forms, woman and man, vary subtly in geometry and chemistry. They draw from the same stream of life in ways that cannot be separated from one another but yet are not quite alike. Despite the closeness, the two genders inherit different outlooks and experiences from the same underlying force, neither side complete. The scheme of human life is both magical and terrifying. On the one hand, it creates an imperative that drives us to break down the walls of individual isolation but at the same time sentences us to a search for completion that may never be fulfilled.

Physical realities delineate existence, however grand the snow-flakes that crystallized from them. The visible forms embed hidden simplicity: birth, death and gender interpretations of life. We hunger to be known through the eyes of a complement. The physical bits and pieces of us will linger when we are gone, but our spirit must be passed like a baton—one-to-one.

The physical experience of pushing horizon to horizon to horizon has heightened my awareness of simple forces and made the pretences and facades of scripted life less bearable for me. Polite and pointless conversation seems like a waste of valuable time. Polarity has been magnified—chemical charges intensified. When all that is sensible is stripped away, I want to discover the simplest resonance that exists in a woman: the awareness of direct connection—plus to minus, short-circuiting. The honesty of attraction—of simple unguided forces—can I allow this vulnerability? Where is the woman who has disassembled life into its basic forces so completely that she will show me her undeniable intentions? The test is in the mutual spontaneity of it.

Goodbye Las Vegas, crucible of simple truths. I have reached Mountain Springs Summit: 5,493 feet above sea level and about 3,500 feet above Las Vegas.

A deep cut slashes into the ridge at the summit, and I swing to the south side of the highway to absorb the view from the shade of this wound. Ahead of me sprawls a series of parallel mountain ranges that cascade, one after another, like a set of waves extending all the way to the Pacific Coast and Santa Barbara. I cannot see them all, but I know they are there—and that I must ride sideways, up and over the backs of each of them. My line of sight extends only as far as the high ridges that outline Death Valley: the Amargosa Range and the still higher Panamint Range. Beyond, the fog of great distance partially veils a few points of the White Mountains and Sierra Nevada. In my mind's eye, I can see the Temblor, Sierra Madre and Santa Ynez ranges rising from intervening desert basins. And of course, between the ocean and me sprawl the great desert valleys including the Mojave, Death Valley, Panamint Valley, and the parched southern tip of San Joaquin Valley.

As hardened as I am by my experience, it is difficult not to be daunted by the vastness and the unforgiving nature of the route beyond. Crossing the remaining expanse would be a nontrivial undertaking in a good car. It is hard to convey the feeling of standing here on the first of these summits that has taken several hours to climb in stifling heat, imagining the trek ahead of me. The Mountain Springs Summit is arguably the most formidable point along a journey that has been laced with formidable points.

I have learned not to dwell in these moments. I push on. After a long, but quick, downhill sail from the summit, I begin working my way over the ups and downs of the highly eroded terrain. Late in the afternoon, a fellow in a car stops beside me. He is a truck driver who passed me several times during the day and observed my toil. He lives in Pahrump, the next town that I will reach, about sunset. It is the first little town I will encounter since leaving Las Vegas. He says I can camp in his back yard and gives directions to his house at the edge of the tiny town. He will put out a hose so I can have water, as well.

It's a good offer. Otherwise, I would have to bivouac in the open desert off the highway, without additional water. I find his house at dusk and park in back. The man comes out for just a few minutes but doesn't talk long. He is divorced and has an adult son who lives with him. The son will come home late, he advises. He himself will leave for work before the dawn. I don't think he has lent his help to be social but is merely giving aid to a traveler in a hostile land. I thank him, and he goes back inside. The lights go out early in the house. I sleep on soft grass rather than coarse rocks because of the kindness of another stranger who, like the others, took nothing in return.

Total mileage for the day: 87.0

## Day 62:

I heard the son come home late, but I did not hear the truck driver leave in the darkness. I loaded *Intrepid*, pushed it onto the road, and pointed it towards Shoshone, the last little dot on the map before reaching Death Valley. The rising sun peeked under a deck of high clouds, then disappeared behind it. The air was blustery and whipped from the north, with a trace of volatility that hinted at the slide of one season into another. For the moment, it was relatively cool, but too windy to be pleasant. Unlike Arches, Canyonlands, and the Grand Canyon, I had never been to Death Valley. I was curious, even excited, to cycle into a dominion with such mystique and a foreboding name.

Nevada stumbled into California in a place no sane person would claim. I cranked over the north end of the Nopah Range, a series of bumps not tall enough to form a horizon of their own. I churned through Shoshone, gone in a blink even on the back of a bicycle. I bent right on California Route 127 and stared down the length of the Green Water Range to the blunt southern end of the much higher Funeral Mountains. Over the tops of the Green Water Range, I also saw the rocky spine of the Black Mountains that form the eastern wall of Death Valley at its southern end. I was beginning to get a sense of the immensity of Death Valley even before I arrived. It took not a couple of mountain ranges to corral it, but required a legion of peaks lined up in a succession of ranges to contain it.

I yanked left on California Route 178 and climbed over a pass at the tail of the Green Water Range. I saw little evidence that these mountains had water of any color, whatsoever. I went down and across a dry valley and then wrestled my way to the top of the more signifi-cant Salsbury Pass, which yielded to me at 3,315 feet. The view at the top stopped me short and sent a shiver through me.

To say that this pass is isolated does not convey the loneliness of the spot, nor the bewilderment. I had not seen a vehicle on the road since leaving Pahrump. The wind moaned with a low howl that filled the spaces inside me and made me feel like it was blowing through my ribs. The road dipped into the distance until it just disappeared, both in front and behind. I could see down the whole back of the Black Mountains and could peer across the valley through a gap in the lava-boned ridgeline to the truly enormous Panamint Range, crowned with a splash of snow on Telescope Peak. In the great distance was the high Sierra Nevada, tearing off the horizon before its natural end.

*Descending into Death Valley*

But it was not just the heights that arrested my breath. It was also the obvious depths. The land was askew—tilted downward dramatically over such an expanse it almost compelled me to put out my hand in front of me for balance to keep from pitching forward. The high horizon magnified the downward tilt and created the illusion that everything was sliding towards the bottom. I could have easily believed that Hell was out there gobbling everything that tumbled down the slope.

All the land I traversed over the past day and a half had certainly been arid and desolate, but I kept discovering bleaker and bleaker shades to the color of desolation. The yellows and scattered pale greens first faded to grays. Then the fuzzy grays eroded to dingy whites and dirty tans of a crumbled rock skin, streaked by the reddish brown scars of ancient lava flows like the earth had bled out and dried in the sun.

More than any I had crossed before, I stood at the edge of a vastness that could swallow you whole. And I was entering through its lonely back door.

I plowed down the incline into the park and then bounced over Jubilee Pass at 1,280 feet. I rolled down—way down—winding towards zero, and below. The road ran out of room to go down on a westward track. So it bent north and tumbled some more but with less ferocity than before. Eventually, I had to pedal again. I was stuck in the pit. The sun had long since vaporized the high deck of clouds. The air was thick and compressed, and the sun reflected from bare rock to heat it from below as well as above.

Thirty miles north of the bend in the road, I encountered the ocean—or so it smelled. This was Badwater, the lowest point in the United States at 282 feet below sea level. Any direction would be uphill from here. I imagined a slit suddenly cut at this level from here to the Pacific, 160 miles away as an arrow would fly. A tidal wave would bore in, almost thirty stories high. I imagined the sea that would be created here and how high up on the mountain behind me it would be.

*Badwater—lowest point in the United States*

Badwater was perfectly still, smoother than glass. The northern breezes of morning had long since died in ranges around the open casket of the great valley. The water's surface shone with the brilliance of the radiant blue sky. Only if you looked almost straight down into the water, with the sun off to your side, could your vision penetrate to the shallow bottom along the edge of the brine. Badwater was clear, no silt being stirred into it by even the tiniest of flows, but with a slightly green tint from whatever was dissolved. Around the edge of the large pool was a wide furrowed brow of white crystals left by evaporation during deeper days in the past. So strong was the brew of Badwater that it smelled more of the ocean than the ocean itself.

Across the landlocked sip of a sea, a hundred yards wide, and up a towering slope that was elevator steep stood the snow-sprinkled top of Telescope Peak, barely ten miles distant and two and a quarter miles over my head—its twin standing upside down in the pool below my feet.

At Badwater, I met the flow of tourists head on. It was not a flood, just a trickle, probably filtering down from Furnace Creek, still almost twenty miles ahead. These were not the Grand Canyon kind of tourists who buy plastic souvenirs and brag-that-I-was-there T-shirts. No, this was a quieter, more attentive-to-the-subtle-details kind of tourist that I really didn't mind. At Badwater, and again on the road to Furnace Creek, vehicles slowed beside me for occupants to hand me cold sodas. Also, all the drivers, even of motorhomes, were respectful and gave me more of the road than I needed.

I pulled into Furnace Creek Campground just before sunset. There were many campers, almost all of them in motorhomes. But there was plenty of room. I pulled up to an empty table, leaned *Intrepid* against the end, sat on the top with my feet on the bench, and killed a canteen. I got up from my throne long enough to find the nearest faucet and poured another canteen over my head. It was still pretty hot at sunset. I would dispense with the tent.

In the pink glow that trailed the end of the day, I sat on the table looking at all the motorhomes and feeling the relative vacuum of simplicity in the space where I sat. The moment felt a lot like the day when I set up my first camp at Capital Reef, when I realized how far I was from home with no vehicle and only what I could carry in my small bags. Over the weeks, I became accustomed to the lightness of my load and the brevity of my means. Now, I was simply amazed that I had been able to come so far and do so much with my simple rig—farther and more than I had expected.

The childlike vision that whirled in my head while riding the bike paths of Austin—of stringing many shorter rides into a longer one—orbited in my mind once again. I had now done what my intuition had told me was possible: that ordinary things stacked end-to-end can sum to something extraordinary if guided by imagination.

There was nothing extraordinary about me. I had just done what I had imagined.

Total mileage for the day: 88.1

*Day's end at Furnace Creek, Death Valley*

## Day 63:

After sunrise, I located the showers and indulged. Then I biked the twenty-six miles to Stovepipe Wells before the heat became unbearable. By afternoon, the day was searing even though it was now into October. I knew the name Death Valley was no joke. It was, instead, a well deserved reputation. If the universe is dwindling towards heat death as Helmholtz proclaimed, the process could surely be deferred by tapping Stovepipe Wells for a reserve supply of thermal energy.

I sat in the shade at the store until most of the day had passed overhead, and then I cranked uphill, eight miles to Emigrant Campground.

Total mileage for the day: 33.9

## Day 64:

I leave in the darkness, perhaps an hour before the morning twilight would begin. The last quarter moon lays an eerie yellow glow on the roadway lighting my slow waltz up the steep incline through Emigrant Canyon towards Wildrose Pass. The sun rises long before I can make the summit at 5,547 feet, twenty-seven miles into my ride. I have not seen a single vehicle during the entire morning.

At Wildrose Pass, I complete an elongated half-circuit to the backside of Telescope Peak, opposite where I mentally vaulted its heights at Badwater. The backside conjures feelings of being hidden or even lost. It's the outback to the outback, the remotest of all. I try to imagine a fictitious sightline bored from where I stood in the salt air at Badwater: angling up and over the reflecting pool; penetrating the mountain less than half-way up to the snow on the summit; boring through the solid rock at its core; then barely jumping back into the air at the road cut, a few feet from where I stand—there to here. It is like trying to imagine a direct trip to China, underneath my feet and upside down.

The area on this side of Telescope Peak is wetter and greener and sprinkled with the colors of flowers. Perhaps it's just the high elevation. Or maybe the west-facing orientation of the tall slopes allows them to capture moisture from the Pacific winds. I try to imagine how the thirsty slopes can be constantly quenched. Water from snowmelt and rains probably percolates into the soil and filters beneath the ground, being stored within the mountain. Then, the groundwater might be slowly wrung out by gravity around the margins of impervious layers of rock that keep it from seeping further down.

I coast down from the pass to the road junction five miles ahead, the narrow road curling and weaving to straighten the undulations in the mountain grade. I detour to the left for a moment to check out Wildrose Campground and fill a canteen. Then I turn and ride back past the junction and out the secret corridor of Wildrose Canyon.

I'm dragged by gravity on a steep ride to a twin hell: the Panamint Valley that parallels its famous brother named Death, one mountain range over. Unlike its twin, Panamint has no settlements, no stores, and no ranger outposts. It is more deserted than Hell. I am riding towards Trona, a small dot on the map along one of the few passages out of Hell. I see no trees, little shrub, and no water—good or bad.

About twenty miles from the park boundary, I am buzzed by a jet fighter that passes directly over my head, so close that I can see the joints in the metal panels that connect to form its skin. I'm not sure, but the pilot may have been more surprised to see me than I was to see him. I could almost hear him telling his buddies that night, "You know what? Today I zapped a bicycle being ridden out of the heart of Hell!"

I ride through Trona, not stopping—amazed that anyone would live here. I see kids playing, and wonder what it would be like to grow up in the suburbs of Hell. Some kind of big rotating tube extends over the road. It rumbles with loud grinding noises as if something is being tumbled and tortured inside. There must be mining of the dry lakebed. I am amazed at what humans will do and call it life.

Beyond Trona, I climb steep switchbacks swinging up a high ridge, look back to the Panamint twin—and say goodbye to Hell.

*Climbing out of the Panamint Valley—*
*but still engulfed by desert*

But I have only ascended one level, to Purgatory. Redemption is still over fifty miles away: through China Lake and Inyokern; and along the little gray-line highway off 395, towards Walker Pass and the Sierra—leading, I hope, to something friendlier beyond.

The sunset closes on me as I pedal into Inyokern. I stop for the largest iced soda I can buy, and then I am gone. Darkness is rising quickly when I hit US Route 395, four miles beyond. This is a big red-line highway with a constant stream of trucks and cars including heavy eighteen-wheelers that shake me as they blast past. I know that I am in harm's way. The crush of darkness is pouring rapidly across the valley, and I am trying to escape. But the uphill road forces me to a low gear. The junction with California 178 crouches below fading silhouettes only three miles ahead. It's dark when I turn. I claw uphill on 178 towards the pass, maybe only a mile or so. I see a river of headlights passing below.

There are scattered shrubs to both sides of the road: hard plants with big spikes that would hurt to rub. I carry *Intrepid* and its load over my right shoulder and pick my way around bayonets, stopping about a hundred yards from the road. Coyotes scream at me from all around. I hear a few of them scurry in the darkness. I growl, and I mean it. They'd better leave me alone! I pitch my tent in the dark and lay *Intrepid* at the door. I couldn't ride to redemption—but I don't think it's far.

Total mileage for the day: 105.2

## Day 65:

The shrieks and growls of the semis, rising from the main highway below, pierce my sleep before the sun gets the chance. The sky is brightening but not yet blue. I strike my tent, pack my load, hoist what I would normally ride, and carry it to the road. I crest Walker Pass at 5,250 feet as the eastern horizon spins below the sun. I stand in the golden rays for a moment and then dive into the long shadow of the mountain ridge.

The slopes on either side of the highway are covered with trees. There are flowers and grasses. Even without looking, change is obvious. The smell of the land has changed: the tickle of spices instead of the choke of dust. And sounds have changed. The silence was so severe yesterday that I could hear my own pulse. Today, I hear the chatter of birds, the buzz of insects, some rustling in the leaves, and of course, an occasional car.

Some driveways of homes clip the winding highway here and there, the type of homes found on the fringes: domes, A-frames, and chalets like those I saw near Ouray and Ridgeway in the mountains of Colorado, and then again on the ride to Mountain Springs Summit outside of Las Vegas.

Soon, I am riding along Isabella Lake, to the right side of the road. Isabella is big and looks deep and silver-blue—a real lake where people fish, ride in boats, and jump in to keep cool. Bodfish, near the end of the lake, is just another dot-like circle on my map but has the trappings of a real town. There is even a freeway-type bypass, but I choose the slow-road through town. I stop at a small store with a porch and a weathered look and find orange juice in the cooler at the back, behind all the tackle and fishing supplies.

At this point, I had zigzagged my way beyond the last fold in the map. Between swigs on the bottle, I turn the map in the clear pocket on the top of my handlebar bag to the side with the ocean and Santa Barbara along one edge, being careful not to disturb the photo of Barbara. I study my options and then decide to abandon the highway for a gray-line on the map that is so skinny it's not even numbered. But it's headed my way.

It's a curvy road, narrow, with no shoulder, and not even a stripe. But there aren't many cars. The good road surface accentuates the peacefulness and charm of the park-like route. Contorted broad-leafed trees wave their branches close up, sometimes hanging over the road. Tall grasses, not quite green but more pleasant than bare rock, crowd the meadows. The shallow, gently rounded mountain valley conveys the feeling of being forgotten and left behind: an unnumbered surprise and good find.

I am cruising in California using middle gears. California has a different feel—electric even in its hidden and forgotten parts. This is where I am going to stay. The thought starts to sink in.

After about twenty-five miles, the road bumps over a short hill where the high valley comes to an end. Here, a sharp kink in the road tops a twisting set of switchbacks that heads down the steep slope. At the point of the kink, before the descent, perches a tree-shaded turnout with some good sitting rocks and a sprawling view. Of course, I stop. Sometimes, a good turn in the road dictates lunch.

I reckon I am at the southern end of a high rim bordering the tip of the San Joaquin Valley. Out there in the distance, at the bottom of the valley, I should be seeing Bakersfield. All I can see is a steely gray-blue cloud. No trace of the city itself is visible. It should be right in front of me, but it is not. The cloud is too thick. This is California? The thought starts to sink in. Okay, I'm glad Bakersfield is not my destination.

Perhaps the cloud below is doing me a favor. The overlook is pleas-ant and there is no city visible to mar the view. It gives me the feeling of being far away. I have the place all to myself. I haven't seen a car for over an hour. I filled two extra canteens in Bodfish, so I indulge in a quick shower.

Reluctantly, I leave the overlook and continue my ride. I dance down the switchbacks, sacrificing the view—then ride through a dot named Caliente and join the double red line that marks the freeway-like California Route 58 for a few miles. I exit at California 223 and head west towards Arvin, south of Bakersfield. I descend on smooth road and in my highest gear. I roll off the slopes and into the flat agricultural land. But I only shift down one notch, still flying. Then, a flat tire near Arvin grounds me for repairs. As I fixed my bike, I see workers tending fields—riding in the back of pickups, stopping, hopping in and out, and crossing the road from time to time. They are fussing with smoking smudge pots that line the fields. Maybe these are the sources for much of the cloud.

I don't want to stick around to test the effects of the smoke from whatever they are burning. I right *Intrepid*, and I am gone—flying once more. I go through Arvin, and by Weed Patch, and then under the freeway California 99—wheels humming. The sunset is coming and I don't want to stay in this chemical cloud for the night. I am not sure where I can stop, anyway. So I am racing, back into high gear even on the flatland. I turn left on an unnumbered road that seems to go the right direction. The roads are laid out squarely and are somewhat predictable along here. Interstate 5 is converging to my right. I don't know if I can get to the other side. But the little road passes beneath the freeway, and I continue the race with the sun. I don't have a plan and don't know where I will stop. I just don't like where I am and figure I need to be somewhere ahead.

The little road bangs into the gray-line of California 166 at a distance where the roar of the Interstate has faded to a murmur. I turn west, towards mountains that now hide the sun. I bike to the brink of darkness and then get another flat tire a couple of miles short of Maricopa. Since I am not going to fix it in the dark, I guess I now have a plan. I go off the road a hundred yards and pitch my tent among the wailings of coyotes and the squeaks and rumbles of bobbing pumps, plunging a field of oil wells. At least I am out of the cloud.

Total mileage for the day: 130.8

## Day 66:

I pitched my tent between two pumping wells, maybe 250 feet apart. I must have incorporated their clanking into my dreams because I woke up feeling like a machine. I fixed the flat tire before I tore down my tent, and then packed my gear and carried *Intrepid* to the road. The store in Maricopa was not yet open, so I waited a few minutes for my morning fueling of orange juice. I patched a spare tube while I waited, hoping not to need it. Immediately south of Maricopa, I started to climb—up the Grocer Grade to 2,968 feet, more than 2,500 feet above Bakersfield. As soon as I began climbing, I started feeling separation from the deserts. There was not yet much physical separation because I could still see the parched San Joaquin over my shoulder. But the mental separation was quick and powerful. I could feel Santa Barbara and the ocean tugging on me.

A few miles ahead, I turned south along California 33. The first of the coastal ranges reared right in front of me. Not long afterwards I saw the sign, "Entering Santa Barbara County." I told myself I was in the neighborhood, at last. I tried not to be impatient, but the tug was getting stronger. It would be hard to explain my feelings as I let the words, "Santa Barbara," repeat in my mind. I tried to absorb the meaning of it. It was not yet home, but somehow I knew I was supposed to go there. I felt an attachment although I had never been there. I felt excited and sad all in the same sweep. As so many times before, when a moment is confusing, the pedaling takes over.

Okay, a little further down the road, I exited Santa Barbara County and entered neighboring Ventura County. But that didn't matter. I had clipped the edge. I was circling in, like I circled in on the Grand Canyon. Only now, the circle was much smaller. I would be there, soon.

I pedaled into the Los Padres National Forest, heading steadily uphill. Then I assaulted a set of switchbacks bulldozed with serious gradient. The afternoon was sunny, hot and perfectly still, and I had to wipe the heavy sweat from my forehead to keep it from running into my eyes. It was a low gear climb in places. I seldom used low gear anymore because my legs had become so strong. But I was glad the switchbacks and the dramatic grade were here and that the view behind me was becoming so wide and so grand. I kept thinking, "Santa Barbara has an outback, right around the corner." The quietness and the solitude of this beautiful stretch of forestland amazed me. It was so close to the city, yet it felt so far away. Whatever I was thinking when I picked Santa Barbara from the almanac, I was certainly getting confirmation from my low-gear, high-sweat reconnaissance.

I leveled out on Pine Mountain Summit at 5,048 feet above sea level and about 4,500 feet higher than where I began the day. The view behind me was beautiful and impressive. But it may have seemed more so because I could still imagine the chilling view back at Mountain Springs Summit, looking across hundreds of miles of deserts and all the high ridges yet to be crossed, pointed towards here. I took a long last look and started rolling towards the ocean.

*Starting the winding descent into Wheeler Gorge*

I took my time crossing the Los Padres backcountry, stopping for a late lunch and a canteen shower. The road slanted much more down than up, and I was beginning to think that most of my work was done. There were many beautiful opportunities to stop and camp. While I considered it, something in me wanted the ride to be done—not because I was weary of riding, but because the refrain "Santa Barbara" had stirred a need for a new connection to be spun. And I figured I could camp here another time since this was Santa Barbara's outback, and I wouldn't have far to go. So, I pushed along.

I approached Wheeler Gorge, and the road bent downward more sharply as well as back and forth upon itself, over and over. As I tacked to and fro down the switchbacks, a powerful sensation overwhelmed—

literally seized—my entire being. I flashed back to the many events of my long journey, seeing them as vividly as when I was there. I didn't just see them; I also *felt* them—not the strain and the sweat of them, but the emotion of them. And I saw them all at once, like they were all happening at the same time. But in the same instant, I also recognized and recalled each place and time separately and distinctly.

So powerful was the vision that it was hard to concentrate to guide my bike on the fast sweeps of the switchbacks. I tried to snap my attention back to me, but this was not in my control. It felt like the stories that are told about one's life flashing before them as they die. I didn't know what was happening, but the experience was completely involuntary and left me giddy for a moment.

There are connections buried deep within us, connections that usually escape our awareness but affect us profoundly. We are connected to the beginning, and we are connected to the end. We are connected to the largest things strung across space and the smallest particles within atoms. We are connected to schemes that we did not invent and cannot control.

And we are strongly connected as women and men by the universal scheme of polarity—the compulsion to complete and be completed. Against the large and seemingly indifferent universe from which we sprang and into which we will disappear, a person may find a sense of personal destiny in the arms of another, marking the uniqueness of each other's existence.

The universe is unwinding. Nothing will last forever. Along the drift to oblivion are the brief splashes of life. Life does not need an external sanction to make it special. The sanction of life is in the rareness of it and in the extraordinary detail of it. The sanction of life is also in the experience of it—the temporariness of it; something that *must* be used. Even a futile cause can be lent meaning by the intimate sharing of it.

The Second Law of Thermodynamics and the expansion of the universe dig gardens as well as graves. While tapping out the march towards death, these mysterious cogs in the physical scheme also motivate the engaging tick of clocks and the creative forces that allow galaxies and life to organize. Wherever there is a vacuum, there is also the opportunity to fill it creatively.

Life is destined to be bittersweet. The meaning, if any, is what you make it. The vacuum of riding alone has created this understanding daily.

Life is short. But for sixty-six days, my life has been immediate and intensely real. I sorted what matters from what doesn't. It has felt like a lifetime and has prepared me for another.

I coasted into Ojai thinking Santa Barbara was not far. I actually saw my first sign to Santa Barbara and got all excited: twenty-eight more miles! I didn't realize that I wasn't going to just roll right down to the ocean. Instead, I found Casitas Reservoir and the climb over one last pass.

By the time I completed this climb, the sun dipped close to the proverbial sinking into the sea. My isolation would end soon, but a profound sadness swept through me. Although simplified, streamlined, and primed for possibilities, I counted some losses. I longed for Barbara, impossible Barbara. I would write to her again—think about her wistfully; imagine the taste of her kiss and the warmth of her embrace, never experienced—then cover the seed she created, somewhere out of consciousness but never forgotten.

The road to Santa Barbara met the beach in Carpinteria. I tucked *Intrepid* into a motel room and walked to the beach. I pictured having dinner with a friend, maybe celebrating a little since Santa Barbara lay only eleven miles way. I stood outside a restaurant for a few minutes but never went in. Celebrating would have to wait for a while—until I found a *new* friend.

Total mileage for the day: 87.1

**Day 67:**

A seed can cradle the germ of life for a long time.

I bicycled the final eleven miles into Santa Barbara. A vacuum waited there for me to fill it.

Total number of miles bicycled during the journey: 2,509

*The Santa Barbara coast and the Channel Islands beyond*

# 15. Trip Log

N.R. = Not Recorded  CG. = Campground  N.P. = National Park
Note: Trip total kept by cumulative odometer (miles by bicycle only)

| Day | Trip Mileage | Total | Campsite | Comments |
|---|---|---|---|---|
| 1 | 38.9 | 38.9 | Along Utah 68 | Flight to Utah; Camped in ditch |
| 2 | 37.7 | 76.6 | Motel in Orem | Back into city; Fixed damage to bike |
| 3 | 87.8 | 164 | Along Utah 28 | Camping off the road with the coyotes |
| 4 | 51.1 | 215 | Along Utah 24 | First picnic table bivouac |
| 5 | 45.5 | 261 | Capitol Reef N.P. | First mountain pass, 8,345 ft. |
| 6 | Hike | | Capitol Reef N.P. | Lookout Point |
| 7 | 9.3 | 270 | Capitol Reef N.P. | Goosenecks Overlook |
| 8 | 82.1 | 352 | Lake Powell | Hickman Bridge hike |
| 9 | 55.0 | 407 | Natural Bridges | Ride over Comb Ridge |
| 10 | 21.7 | 429 | Natural Bridges | Hiking, Sipapu and Kachina Bridges |
| 11 | 49.9 | 479 | Devil's Canyon | Manti-La Sal National Forest |
| 12 | 88.3 | 567 | Arches N.P. | |
| 13 | Hike | | Arches N.P. | Hanging out with Monika & gang |
| 14 | Hike | | Arches N.P. | More hanging out with the gang |
| 15 | 29.7 | 597 | Cane Springs | Roadside park along U.S. 191 |
| 16 | 67.4 | 664 | Canyonlands N.P. | Squaw Flat CG. |
| 17 | 6 | 670 | Canyonlands N.P. | Chesler Park hike |

| Day | Trip Mileage | Total | Campsite | Comments |
|---|---|---|---|---|
| 18 | 6 | 676 | Canyonlands N.P. | Confluence Overlook hike |
| 19 | 53.2 | 729 | Motel | Uphill to Monticello, Utah |
| 20 | 66.3 | 795 | Motel | U.S. 666 to Cortez, Colorado |
| 21 | 25.8 | 821 | Along U.S. 160 | Thompson Park CG., San Juan N.F. |
| 22 | 72.3 | 893 | Motel | U.S. 550 to Farmington, New Mexico |
| 23 | 36.9 | 930 | Along N.M. 44 | U.S. 64 east; New Mexico 44 south |
| 24 | 49.3 | 979 | Chaco Canyon | Dirt road New Mexico 57 to park |
| 25 | N.R. |  | Chaco Canyon | Hiking and biking; Tsin Kletsin |
| 26 | N.R. |  | Chaco Canyon | Hiking and biking; Pueblo Alto |
| 27 | N.R. | 1,048 | Chaco Canyon | Hiking and biking; Eileen arrives |
| 28 | Drive |  | Mesa Verde N.P. | Back to Colorado by car with Eileen |
| 29 | 19.8 | 1,068 | Purgatory CG. | Resumed ride starting in Durango |
| 30 | 34.1 | 1,102 | Along U.S. 550 | Bivouac at Red Mountain Pass |
| 31 | 65.1 | 1,167 | Sunshine CG. | San Juan N.F., Colorado |
| 32 | 42.2 | 1,209 | Forks CG. | Confluence of Dolores & W. Dolores |
| 33 | 23.9 | 1,233 | Motel | Cortez, Colorado |
| 34 | 145.9 | 1,379 | Monument Valley | Two broken spokes; U.S. 160 into AZ |
| 35 | 14.1 | 1,394 | Monument Valley | Ride/push bike around dirt loop |

Trip Log

177

| Day | Trip Mileage | Total | Campsite | Comments |
|---|---|---|---|---|
| 36 | 162.4 | 1,556 | Sunset Crater | U.S. 160 & U.S. 89 into pine forest |
| 37 | Walk | 1,556 | Sunset Crater | Write; let sore knee recover |
| 38 | 41.1 | 1597 | Pine Flat CG. | Lowell Observatory; Oak Creek Canyon |
| 39 | 54.0 | 1651 | Clear Creek CG. | Restless night in the Arizona desert |
| 40 | 0 | 1651 | Clear Creek CG. | Layover in the shade of big trees |
| 41 | 41.9 | 1693 | Clint's Well CG. | Coconino N.F., Arizona |
| 42 | 50.5 | 1743 | Off roadway | Camped near Flagstaff airport |
| 43 | 83.1 | 1826 | Ten-X CG. | Kaibab N.F.; passed Humphrey's Peak |
| 44 | N.R. | | Mather CG. | Walk-in CG. at Grand Canyon N.P. |
| 45 | N.R. | | Horseshoe Mesa | Overnight backpack into Grand Canyon |
| 46 | N.R. | | Mather CG. | Rim riding at Grand Canyon |
| 47 | N.R. | | Mather CG. | Rim riding; Letter from Barbara |
| 48 | N.R. | | Mather CG. | South Kaibab Trail to near river |
| 49 | N.R. | | Mather CG. | Rim Riding at Grand Canyon |
| 50 | N.R. | | Mather CG. Canyon | Rim Riding at Grand |
| 51 | N.R. | | Mather CG. | Rim Riding at Grand Canyon |
| 52 | N.R. | | Tanner Rapids | Overnight backpack to Colorado River |

| Day | Trip Mileage | Total | Campsite | Comments |
|-----|-----|-----|-----|-----|
| 53 | N.R. | | Mather CG. | Rim riding at Grand Canyon |
| 54 | N.R. | | Mather CG. | French film crew at sunset |
| 55 | N.R. | | Mather CG. | Hiked South Kaibab Trail to river |
| 56 | N.R. | | Mather CG. | Rim riding at Grand Canyon |
| 57 | N.R. | 1966 | Mather CG. | Sightseeing with Eileen & Nancy |
| 58 | Hike | | Mather CG. | Hike to Indian Gardens & overlook |
| 59 | Hike | | Hermit Rapids | Overnight backpack to Colorado River |
| 60 | Car | 1966 | Lake Mead | Hike out of canyon in snow & ice |
| 61 | 87.0 | 2053 | Pahrump, Nevada | Resumed ride at lake after jump by car |
| 62 | 88.1 | 2141 | Furnace Creek | Death Valley N.P. |
| 63 | 33.9 | 2175 | Emigrant CG. | Death Valley N.P. |
| 64 | 105.2 | 2280 | Along Calif. 178 | Long ride through Panamint Valley |
| 65 | 130.8 | 2411 | Along Calif. 166 | Camped with oil wells & coyotes |
| 66 | 87.1 | 2498 | Carpinteria | Reality & excitement still sinking in |
| 67 | 11.2 | 2509 | Santa Barbara | Home. . . but not home |

# Order *Spoked Dreams* from the Publisher

*Spoked Dreams* may be ordered directly from the publisher through the mail or over the Internet. Single copies may be purchased for $16.95 each plus $3.00 for postage (within the USA) and packaging. Orders for three or more copies may be purchased for $15.95 per book, and the postage (within the USA) will be paid by the publisher. Orders shipped to Texas addresses must add 8.25% sales tax.

Visit **www.spokeddreams.com** for online ordering and for color images of the *Spoked Dreams* adventure. The Website also includes general information on bicycle touring and specific routes.

NOTE: This page may be photocopied and used as a mail order form. Prices are subject to change without prior notice. Check **www.spokeddreams.com** for current prices.

Number of books _____ @ $ _____ each + Tax &
shipping _____ = Total enclosed $ _____
Name: _____
Street Address: _____
City: _____
State: _____ZIP Code: _____
Email or phone: _____
Payment: ❑ Check    ❑ Money Order
         ❑ Visa    ❑ MasterCard
For payment by credit card:
Card holder name: _____
Account number: _____
Card expiration date: _____/ _____
Signature: _____

NOTE: Air-Space Press does not share confidential information and destroys credit card numbers after the transaction is completed.

Send orders to:
**Air-Space Press**
P.O. Box 152739
Austin, Texas 78715-2739